HENRI SZEPS was born in Switzerland in 1943 and came to Australia when he was eight. He studied drama with Hayes Gordon between 1962 and 1966 while completing science and electrical engineering degrees at Sydney University. Since then he has worked extensively in television and theatre both in Australia and the UK. He is probably best known for his TV role of Robert in *Mother and Son*. Other credits include the film *Travelling North*, the TV drama series *Palace of Dreams* and, on stage, *The Good Doctor*, *Glengarry Glen Ross*, *Sky* and the world premieres of David Williamson's *Travelling North*, *Dead White Males* and *Heretic*.

For Mary Ann, Amos and Josh

ALL IN GOOD TIMING

A Personal Account of What an Actor Does

HENRI SZEPS

Illustrations by Peter Meldrum

Currency Press • Sydney

First published in 1996
by Currency Press Ltd,
PO Box 452, Paddington,
NSW 2021, Australia

Copyright © Henri Szeps, 1996

9 8 7 6 5 4 3 2 1 0

This book is copyright. Apart from any fair dealing for the purpose of private study, research or review, as permitted under the Copyright Act, no part may be reproduced by any process without written permission. Inquiries concerning publication, translation or recording rights should be addressed to the publishers.

NATIONAL LIBRARY OF AUSTRALIA – CIP DATA

Szeps, Henri.
   All in good timing : a personal account of what an actor does.
   ISBN 0 86819 484 0.
   1. Szeps, Henri. 2. Acting. I. Title
792.028

Printed by Australian Printing Group, Maryborough, VIC.

FRONT COVER: (clockwise from top left) with Derek Jacobi, Prospect Theatre Co., 1973–4; with Colin Croft, *Good Doctor*, Ensemble Theatre, 1975; *The Double Bass*, Ensemble Theatre, 1991; with Ruth Cracknell, *Mother and Son*, ABC; publicity shot for *The Double Bass*, in the Playhouse, Victorian Arts Centre, 1991; as Rocco Bettoni, *Sky*, Ensemble Theatre, 1992; on set, filming *Travelling North*, 1986.

CONTENTS

Foreword by Leo McKern   *vii*
Preface   *ix*

1	Why do we Act?	1
2	Comedy	3
3	Timing	17
4	Acting	24
5	Playing Actions	36
6	Motivation	44
7	Objects of Actions and Adjustments	55
8	The Script	67
9	Rehearsals	81
10	Characterisation	102
11	Meet the Audience	115
12	Film & Television	128
13	Long Runs	138
14	Warm Up	147

Appendix: List of Actions   *157*
Index   *159*

FOREWORD

Leo McKern

I once wrote 'Books about acting are either boring or silly' (*Just Resting* 1983). The first word should have been 'many' and I should have certainly excepted Konstantin Stanislavsky's *An Actor Prepares* which remains a sort of Bible for the profession.

This book of Henri Szeps' is neither silly nor boring, but informative, entertaining, provocative, and above all, very brave. Not so much a Bible, as Baedecker, an intensely personal guidebook to what makes one actor (a very good actor indeed) tick.

Michael Redgrave once said that he did not trust instinctive actors; it may well have been in his book on acting, or I may have heard it in his presence, I don't remember. But being fortunate enough to have been a member of an Old Vic Company season which he led and witnessing the way he worked, I saw what he meant. In that season, in which he played Hamlet, Berowne, Rakitin and Young Marlow, I still consider that he was at his peak; every character was superbly done. It was his method to build a character like a West Country mason building a dry-stone wall, stone by perfectly fitting stone, which even without mortar will last for centuries.

But for him to discount instinctive acting so easily disturbed me, admiring him so much as I did. (He was extremely kind to me, and enormously encouraging.) I could not, having never been trained, imagine acting in any other way; I certainly could not discuss or dissect the subject into words as he did. Henri Szeps has the capacity to do just that; to lay out the whole approach to his work as an actor. This is a considerable feat, particularly in a profession (if I may call it that) the vast majority of whose members' attempting such a task would result in what I have already opined as boring or silly.

Stanislavsky suggests an exercise which I still find fascinating to attempt; searching for what he called 'Super-objective'; to define a play or part in a single sentence or phrase, or best of all, one word. Over a long time, the best I could come up with regarding my work was 'A passionately private indulgence that one hopes will be noticed and applauded'. That paradox speaks very well for me.

Henri Szeps is not content with this kind of simpleness, but constructs a very personal, considered analysis of every aspect of his work; and while not seconding his every notion, I cannot but admire his constructive pursuance, in print, of his raison d'etre.

I once heard John Freeman remark in a television *Face to Face* programme with Tyrone Guthrie, 'Surely actors are just showing off?' to which Guthrie replied 'On the contrary ... what they are doing is hiding'. Well, as Gloucester says to Edgar, 'And that's true too'. But hiding, showing off, clowning, miming, attempting to entertain in whatever form requires a basic necessity — talent. Szeps is talented in many directions, and lifts a few curtains for us; and every scene is worth watching.

However, sometimes even talent can be dispensed with, given another gift which may be called 'personality', 'personal magnetism', 'presence' or even an awful bastard word 'watchability'; it can even be a matter of personal beauty, and explains the existence of many 'stars'; but actors, as I understand the word, they are not. But on the rare occasions when talent and presence come together in the one actor, unforgettable things can happen.

I have had the good fortune to have worked with Donald Wolfit at the Old Vic; not for long, alas, for deprived of his own dreadful company, and being directed by others, even Guthrie, was more than he could bear, and he left before the season ended. But Wolfit was, on but rare occasions, a great actor. In a time when the language can be meaningless, over-adjectivised idiocy, I use the word and the phrase in its true sense; he was the only great actor I have seen.

The mother of timing is rhythm, and without a sense of it a great number of things cannot be performed well, and attempting to teach or instil it is as hopeless a task as investing the tone-deaf with perfect pitch. *All In Good Timing* supplied the answer, an explanation, an example (often with a giggle) to practically every query I could think of relating to my business, while remaining a very personal safari across some dangerous ground. But Szeps has made it, and we can sit in the shade and have a beer. I commend this brave book to all the under 75's; if you haven't made it by then, consider, say, chiropody.

PREFACE

The music swells and the lights finally dim right out. The shuffling and whispering cease and the lights on stage come up. A character is reading a letter. She is beautiful, her dress is glamorous, the whole set and lighting are magical. She speaks with ease, confidence and authority. But what is she thinking? What is going on behind the eyes? Why is the piece of paper in her hand trembling ever so slightly? And how does she know when to look up?

There have been many books written about acting, but as far as I know not all that many about timing. Timing is regarded as a taboo. It is elusive, ephemeral, ethereal. It defies analysis and, by conventional wisdom, cannot be discussed.

Sports commentators on the other hand tend to be ex-champions themselves. At Wimbledon, for example, they can see the decoy, they can tell you where the player thought the ball was coming to, which leg her weight was on before she moved, and why she returned it to where she did. The commentators can virtually read the players' minds.

There is very little difference between hitting a good return and timing a good line. They are both deliberate processes. In both cases, at some critical moment, the player knew her intention. In both cases there was a lightning decision to be made. The only reason that timing in the theatre is seldom discussed is because the commentators are rarely actors or comedians themselves. Theatre reviewers, journalists and lecturers of English literature are our commentators. And God bless them for their commitment and love of theatre, but these people are not generally riveting performers themselves. They cannot know what is going on inside the actor's head. Even experienced drama teachers can have little to say about it, unless they have themselves spent years performing that 'micro-surgery in flight', the act of timing an audience. On the other hand few people who survive on good timing like to talk or write about it. Louis Armstrong did not give many public lectures on 'how you know when to slide onto the next note'. So we have a catch-22 situation.

I am an actor. I have enjoyed a very pleasant career in the industry for some 25 years. Because of the amount of comedy that I have been called upon to perform, my attention has become more and more focussed on timing. I also happen to be passionately

analytical, so I thought I might try to break the impasse and put down on paper what it is that I think we do when we time. I am not holding myself up as the greatest exponent of the skill, I am too often wrong and too often uncertain. It does not need a genius to write this — just someone who has first-hand knowledge of the internal processes, and who is interested in describing these to others.

I am not a teacher. I have not had the experience of beginning with a raw novice and three years later sending them out, equipped to tackle the world of showbusiness. I have a fear that if I took up teaching I might begin to believe my own theories and approaches to acting. I would feel I had an onus to keep faith with these theories and that I would cease exploring. To me that would be a disaster. One of the joys of being an artist is the constant challenge of questioning past approaches and seeing if there is not some way of pushing one's own limits, of finding some more accurate way of representing a moment of life. One is always on the look-out to achieve a clearer, simpler truth.

PREFACE

In order to clarify my ideas I began giving occasional one-week courses at the Actors' Centre in Sydney. I have done this over a period of about five years, to get my ideas into some kind of structure and to get a feel for the pupils' needs. Often there seemed to be a desire for a clear overview of what we do and what we try to achieve as actors. There are an awful lot of technical approaches floating about but not many of them seem to have at their heart simple communication and the telling of the story.

The aim of this book is to discuss timing and how this fundamental element flows through all of comedy and drama. The result is an overview, a philosophy, if you like, of acting. Our most common association with timing is of course comedy. For this reason we will have a quick look at what makes us laugh before discussing timing in particular and then acting in general.

An important aspect of writing this book is to share three notions with you which are original: The Behaviour Capsule, Audience Gravity, and Moment by Moment Control. There are no doubt other practitioners in the world who have arrived at parallel concepts, but they are unknown to me, and in the form that the concepts appear here, they are original.

In the spirit that this overall philosophy has helped me I share it with you, whether you be a drama student, an old pro eager for a reappraisal, or a member of the public, intrigued by what happens back-stage, behind an actor's eyes.

1
WHY DO WE ACT?

In my first major commercial production I appeared as Harold, in Mart Crowley's play *The Boys in the Band* in Sydney. This was a sensation in 1968, being about a gay birthday party. My character was a very strong, ice-cold, pockmarked, Jewish gay man, the birthday boy — a wonderful role. We were proud that our production had opened very soon after the original American one and that ours was equally successful. We ended up playing for some 21 months, in the major cities of this vast country. I had studied acting for four years while also gaining Bachelor degrees in Science and Electrical Engineering at Sydney University. I had only been a full-time actor for 18 months when I was thrown into this extraordinary situation of having to play the one role for so long so early in my career. Every night, on with the latex pockmarks (latex is a liquid rubber which as it dries on your skin can be twisted and pulled over itself to create lumps and distortions on the flesh); on with the turquoise Nehru jacket, on with the sunglasses and onto the stage.

After about 18 months of this I was going mad. I had to ask myself the question: What on earth was I doing? Why was I putting on weird make-up, getting dressed in strange clothes, going out in front of a room full of people I'd never met, saying things I didn't mean?

In my attempt to answer these questions I soon realised that I was facing the much deeper ones: What is art? What is culture? Why do we do them? A couple of years later, in England, I came across a book, *Introduction to the Study of Man* by J. Z. Young (Oxford University Press, 1971), which was to become my bible. Dr Young had been professor of anatomy at University College, London. His was a biologist's viewpoint, but he was a poet and a philosopher, and he had the breadth of vision to incorporate science, art and religion into his framework. Suddenly, I saw my vocation as something less than frivolous, as something more than a trivial middle-class distraction. This biologist allowed me to see art and culture as strands fundamental to human survival. Originally myth, ritual, art, music, magic, science, tradition were all interwoven into one intricate web. It was modern society that had separated them out, making a distinction between art, science, religion and law.

Australian Aboriginal rock paintings and the Lascaux cave in France are silent testament to these ancient spiritual activities. I adore the story about Picasso when he first saw the breathtaking 17,000 year old paintings of bison and deer in the cave at Lascaux. He apparently came out of the cave, angrily mumbling 'We have invented nothing!'

The crucial notion for me was this: It is obvious that so long as people with the natures of Leonardo da Vinci, William Shakespeare and Ludwig van Beethoven are born, the world will have paintings, poetry and music. It will have culture which expresses our deepest feelings, and affirms our existence on the planet. What is not so obvious is that every one of us needs these things, to give us a context in which to place ourselves in terms of our fellow humans and in terms of the cosmos.

Since humans first made fires in caves, societies have survived by reaffirming their myths and value systems. Modern societies have the added task of questioning present systems and exploring new models, as the world changes at an ever increasing pace; as technology becomes all-pervasive; and as populations continue to swell. Social values and relationships of every kind are being questioned and readjusted, even as the avenues left to us for survival on the planet begin to look more and more constrained.

More than ever our societies need arenas in which to discuss these notions, the better to know ourselves, so that we may adjust our behaviour. More than ever we need release, escape, enjoyment and the opportunity to laugh at our fears.

What is lovely is that in modern societies all of these needs can be satisfied inside large, cave-like spaces, where people sit huddled together in the dark, watching a lit area, in which some people tell them a story.

That act of watching in itself seems comforting. Rather than confront us, which is what I had long assumed, it is possible that the spectacle actually distracts us from our cares and fears, by showing us *other* people's troubles. The soothing effect could be that the performance deals with our problems without us actually having to face them. Whatever the reason the show seems to form a buffer between ourselves and the cold harsh world. It takes the unruly parameters of life and confines them to a manageable, imaginary world, up there on the stage. Up there, because that world is impotent, because it is man-made, our fears and problems can be given free rein. They can be inspected bravely at close range, and in the case of comedy they can be blown away by laughter.

2
COMEDY

A little show-biz story. Dame Edith Evans is on stage with a dozen other people; the audience is watching. In the middle of a scene everything stops. Nobody speaks. The prompter whispers the line from the side of the stage. Still no one speaks. The prompter repeats the line a little louder; some members of the audience hear it and start to titter; still no one speaks. The prompter finally yells the line out, the audience roars with laughter. As the laughter dies down Dame Edith turns to the prompter and says, 'We know the line, dear, we don't know who says it!'

LAUGHTER

One of the more intriguing pieces of behaviour that we humans exhibit is this strange barking sound when we find something funny. A car back-fires. A split-second later, after the shock, when we discover that the noise was harmless, we laugh. Why?

A little joke: Two six year olds, one rushes up to the other and says, 'Joey, Joey! I found a contraceptive pill on the patio!' Joey says, 'Did you! ... What's a patio?'

We will refer back to this.

Tension

It is commonly acknowledged that laughter is a means of releasing tension. The tension may come from fear, from guilt, from embarrassment, shock or surprise. When the threat turns out to be harmless, we tend to laugh.

Jerry Lewis was giving a lecture on comedy to a group of students at an American college. He was sitting on a chair in front of the class, on a platform about 25 centimetres above the floor. Lewis had carefully placed his chair with its back favouring the audience but at an angle. The leg nearest the audience was placed within a millimetre of the edge of the dais. As he sat, he leaned the whole chair over the edge of the platform on that precarious leg, calmly discussing comedy and how important tension is. The class of course was in fits of laughter as he dangerously flirted with tipping over.

This was a wonderful example of the principle at work. But

consider this: would they still have laughed if he had been teetering on the edge off a cliff, above jagged rocks and pounding waves? The greatest harm that could have come to him in falling off the dais would have been to his dignity. When it comes to real danger, where one faces death or maiming, things cease to be funny.

Comedy is a Threat With the Sting Taken Out

That definition is not original, but as a general statement I have not heard better.

Laughter is a means of lightening our pain, of defusing our fear, of soothing some discomfort or embarrassment. These emotions can be aroused in any one of a million ways, and for countless reasons, but the basic mechanisms of laughter are always the same. A real tension is created, which then turns out not to threaten us here, now, directly.

The two most common factors which create tension in comedy are *surprise* and *discomfort*.

SURPRISE

Charles Chaplin was asked by a student at a film school how he would tell the story. Would he first have a shot of the banana peel on the ground, and then cut to the man walking towards it, who would then slip on it? Or would he first show the man walking towards us, and then cut to the banana peel, and then show the man slipping on it? Chaplin said that he would first show the banana peel. Then he would cut to the man walking towards it. But before the man got to the banana peel he would disappear down a manhole.

The opposite of surprise is boredom. We will have a great deal more to say about surprise throughout this book. It is the fundamental ingredient of all timing.

In order to hold the audience we must never allow them to be able to predict the next moment.

That applies equally to drama as to comedy.

DISCOMFORT

As well as the momentary discomfort created by the surprise itself, there are a number of topics which when touched can cause us unease, and hence tension. We will respond to anything that reminds us of our own ineptness, of our vulnerability or fallibility. Anything that confronts us with our own guilt will generate a little tension which can be released as laughter.

Every comedy situation has someone either embarrassed or humiliated, or threatened to be.

Here is a rough and limited list of things that can make us laugh:

Physical Errors: people fumbling, tripping, falling over.

Verbal Errors: people mispronouncing words, misunderstanding events or orders. We laugh at puns and double entendres.

Social Errors: people unfamiliar with accepted customs, making a *faux pas*, inadvertent unacceptable behaviour, improper manners.

Confusion: people unable to decide on a course of action, or responding inappropriately.

Rejection: someone not accepted by their peers, not admitted into the 'group'.

The 'Other': people who are members of any 'other' class, culture, race, religion or social background. There are two main groups.

Upper — those we want to tear down. Authority figures, such as the police, politicians, priests, mothers-in-law, the boss, anyone pompous or pretentious.

Lower — those we want to distance ourselves from. Anyone we want to regard as inferior, such as foreigners, members of lower classes, certain minorities, the disabled, the insane (and anyone else we can't understand).

Taboos: The most common subjects for comedy (common in both senses of the word) tend to hinge on either sex or the lavatory. These topics are laden with guilt and embarrassment. Other sources of guilt which fall into this group are bigotry and sadism (the sick joke).

It is fair to say that in Western societies when any of these subjects are touched on publicly we are likely to feel a stirring of discomfort, a wisp of anxiety for no apparent reason. Where is the great tragedy in mispronouncing a word or in breaking wind? And yet grown adults will roar with laughter as Lou Costello gets his fingers jammed in a window and when Groucho Marx makes yet another ludicrous pun. Why? Where do these tensions come from?

THE CHILD IN COMEDY

There was a time of course when walking was a very dangerous activity and difficult to learn. When falling over was very likely and speech for the most part was a bewildering stream of gibberish. Words were almost infinite in number and many sounded similar. They were all difficult to pronounce and even harder to learn to string together. It was a time of the most bizarre do's and don'ts, of arbitrary rules that had to be obeyed if you wanted to be accepted and loved. You couldn't scribble on Daddy's papers; you couldn't wee in your pants. Logic had not yet appeared. Brightly coloured butterflies could fly in the air and fish could swim in the water. Everything was possible, arbitrary and jumbled. It was a time of magic, helplessness, love and confusion.

Childhood was also the time when what was being printed into our brains was fundamental; it formed the basis of the people we were going to be. Those memories helped form our attitudes to the world, and our skills and likes and dislikes.

What I am about to say is pure conjecture. But I think that when

Delivering the Punchline

we see Buster Keaton do one of his astounding prat-falls, it is the child in us that is awakened, and frightened, and delighted that it is not us falling over. And when Lou Costello misunderstands an order, it is the child in us that is relieved at not being as stupid as him. I am suggesting that all humour is childhood driven. They are ancient childhood fears and embarrassments that are touched by the things which make us laugh.*

As adults there may be tensions in the work place, say with the boss. We will then welcome humour that thumbs its nose at authority, for example Chaplin outwitting the policeman. However, these adult frustrations don't quite explain the glee that sometimes comes from comedy moments. It seems that the present day frustrations reverberate with much more powerful, parallel feelings from an earlier stage. Frustrations with the boss might resonate with a time of greater defencelessness, perhaps in the face of a very authoritarian father. The joke arouses those old pains, but now from this safe distance, it allows you to laugh at them, and in so doing also relieve today's pains.

---

* Incidentally, has there ever been a better example of word-based comedy than the brilliant Abbott and Costello sketch 'Who's On First?' If you're not familiar with this routine beg, borrow or steal it, but see it and rejoice.

It is not *proof* that comedy is childhood driven but it is persuasive to note that for a great many comedians the language they use, the idioms of behaviour, are those of childhood.

SEX

There seems to be one glaring exception to humour being childhood driven, and that is sex. One of the richest veins in all of comedy seems to go against the principle. The discomfort and guilt associated with sex would seem to emanate from puberty rather than from childhood.

But of course, sexual awareness and exploration begin very early. Perhaps the parents' anxiety about sex is visited upon the infant, as regards touching itself, or the parents' genitalia. Occurring close to the time of toilet training, as these developments do, there might be an association of guilt between these two taboos. I do find it interesting that these two most common sources of humour, are activities which remain glaringly animal. We have been able to camouflage the animalness of other activities. With eating and drinking, for example, we have evolved sophisticated procedures for the preparation of the food and drink, and ceremony associated with its consumption. The whole process of civilisation seems to have been one of us trying to distance ourselves from our animal heritage. But toilet and sex stubbornly sit there as embarrassing reminders.

DEATH

Death is surely the greatest fear that we have. One might then expect it to be the source of the very greatest tension and therefore comedy. It isn't. The humour surrounding death is gentle, dark and wry. Indeed we call it 'black humour'. I can only assume that this is because it is not childhood driven. Children don't fear death. It is not until one's thirties or even forties that the clear, cold knowledge actually forms — that we are not permanent. It is only in mid-life that we begin to catch glimpses of the organic truth that we will die. This is the one great anxiety that has no childhood reverberations. And it is the only one that cannot be easily diffused. There is no joy in death.

THE JOKE

The archetypal 'joke' contains a couple of elements fundamental not only to all of comedy but to timing in general. Timing in drama not only relates to the obvious surprises that the audience is meant to experience, for example from a gun-shot or a sudden twist in the story. Timing relates to every moment of the play. It is the rate at which the information is being delivered which will determine whether or not the audience's attention will be held. The same information mis-timed becomes boring. It will be useful, at this point, to look at the simple anatomy of the joke as a classic example of the juxtaposition of moments.

A joke in its simplest form has three segments: the set-up, the tag, and what I call the hiatus.

The *set-up* — often called the plant, or the feed — points the audience's attention in one direction.

The *tag* — or the switch, or the pay-off — presents the audience with what seems to be a totally unrelated piece of information. It whips the audience's attention into a totally different direction.

The *hiatus* is the ensuing pause before the laugh. It is that dead moment, that split-second of panic in which the audience flounders around trying to link the set-up with the tag, two bits of information which seem miles apart, at opposite ends of our brain. When they make the link the momentary tension created by the confusion is released as laughter.

There is nothing worse for a joke than to analyse it. Forgive me for what follows but I'm afraid this has to be done if we are to become familiar with notions used later. Consider the little joke about Joey earlier (page 3).

The set-up is that Joey's friend has found a contraceptive pill and Joey is enthusiastic — 'Did you!' Then he hesitates. The audience doesn't know why. They are caught a little off-guard. Is he trying to decide what to do with the pill? Or doesn't he know what it is? Was he only playing along with his friend's enthusiasm? When he says 'What's a patio?' the audience is thrown completely off balance. This is the switch. The audience's brains are scrambling around during the hiatus, trying to make sense of things and a tension builds. Once they see the gag — Joey knows what a contraceptive pill is, but not a patio — they laugh.

This is so important that I would like to rephrase it.

The set-up points the audience's minds in one direction. (Joey's excited about the contraceptive pill.) The audience's mental road runs straight ahead. The tag (he doesn't know what a patio is) snaps the audience's brains at right angles. They can't take the sharp corner and become airborne. They fly through the air, scrambling around looking for the link between plant and tag. A tension builds. Once the connection is made and the audience lands safely on the ground having understood the joke, they are relieved, pleased at the recognition, and the tension is released as laughter.

A psychiatrist friend of mine suggests that when the brain is suddenly thrown into that panic state of having to look for the link quickly, it is forced to work so fast that it is effectively thrown into 'fight or flee' mode, which is in itself invigorating, and finally pleasing if resolved.

The Powder Keg

We have mentioned that the laughter often comes from deeper discomforts than what seems to have been immediately addressed. This leads me to the following model of a really good joke.

The switch is like a fuse.

The sensitive, underlying subject matter is like a powder keg.

Making the link between the totally unrelated elements is a first stage. The confusion generates only a small tension. It is only when this energy touches the much deeper, more powerful childhood resonances that the whole thing truly explodes. Because then we are encouraged to defuse far more dangerous problems.

Puns on their own, for example, are not generally all that funny. Yet when they touch a deep nerve they can give rise to hilarity.

THE CLAN

Common Knowledge

The laugh after a joke is a quick response to a momentary surprise. During the hiatus we scramble through our mental data-base to try to find the connection between plant and tag. If we manage to find the link fast enough we will laugh at the joke. But if a necessary piece of information is missing in our information kit the connection cannot be made. If you didn't know what a patio was you would not find the joke funny. That added confusion would prevent you from seeing the joke clearly. Once it was explained you still would not laugh. Just as your hands will not clap if you bring them together slowly so a laugh cannot occur if the connection is not made instantly. This has enormous implications for the nature of humour: *Comedy unites people with like knowledge.*

There is a graffiti that I love, where one person has written: 'God hates homos.' Underneath someone else has written: 'But he loves tabouli!' This joke has no meaning to people not familiar with Lebanese food.

Another popular graffiti in Australia says: 'Australia sux.' Underneath someone else has written: 'New Zealand nil.' That would have no meaning to people not familiar with the subtle difference between how Australians and New Zealanders pronounce six; and the friendly rivalry between the two nations.

Many jokes depend on very specific knowledge, on subtle distinctions. They unite all people who are familiar with these nuances, and exclude the rest. This makes for very strong bonding within the 'clan'. We all get great satisfaction at being part of the in-group that can share and appreciate the joke.

COMMON TASTE

As well as common knowledge, humour unites people who are prepared to laugh at the particular subject matter. Auschwitz jokes don't go over too well at bar mitzvahs, nor do Salman Rushdie jokes at Muslim weddings. When people laugh at a joke they make an unspoken agreement that they belong to the group which is prepared to laugh at this little impropriety. This collusion at breaking a 'taboo' creates both a bond and a tension.

Men will reinforce intimacy by sharing sexually explicit jokes. But by the same token a risqué joke, if sensitively handled, can be the absolute highlight of an elegant dinner party. A breaking-of-the-rules tension is built which, if accepted by all, becomes a very strong bonder.

Every profession, every discipline, every sector of the community has its own in-jokes. The bonding it generates seems to be inversely proportional to the number of people who can understand it. The smaller the number in the 'in-group' the louder the howls of delight. Some groups like to see their humour as definitive, as the most sophisticated.

When very specialised knowledge, or very specific attitudes are required to understand a joke one might be tempted to challenge the notion that humour is childhood driven. After all, a child could not possibly have this specialised information, this degree of sophistication. This misses the point. When a group of nuclear physicists falls about at a mistake in a quantum equation, or a classical orchestra is wetting themselves over a bum note, it is still the child in those people that is vulnerable to the embarrassment. In-humour is not necessarily 'sophisticated'.

Sophisticated humour, I think, depends on how subtly the cues are sent and received. It depends on sensitivity of perception, on depth of understanding of human nature. It can also occur when a whole range of elements of our souls are being touched by the one punch-line. If I may give it a plug, I regard the British television comedy *Yes, Minister* as being at times very sophisticated. Notice that there are no in-jokes here. There couldn't be because viewers don't know the technicalities of how governments work. What they do in the show, which I find astonishing, is to constantly explain the background to a joke as they develop it, and then still manage to get the laugh.

> ### SUMMARY
> Laughter then has at least a three-fold basis:
>
> 1. It releases the tension created by the surprise of the comedy moment itself;
>
> 2. It releases tensions generated by touching on childhood fears and vulnerabilities;
>
> 3. It acts as a signal to those around us that we are part of the clan,
>   a. since we have the necessary information to understand the joke, and
>   b. because we choose to see the subject matter as fit for laughter.

IMPERSONATION, MIMICRY AND CARICATURE

JOIN THE DOTS

At the heart of visual perception is the ability to identify edges. In order to make sense of the profusion of colours, of darkness and light assaulting its eyes, the baby has to learn to decipher the outlines of objects. It could well be that sparse line-sketches, and suggestions, toy with the very fundamentals of visual perception. They tease us by providing the minimum of information needed for us to recognise the required object. A similar process might be what titillates us when we see a caricature, a cartoon or an impersonation. We know that it is false, we know that it is shorthand but it is tantalising to have the real thing generated in such a fashion.

Subtle or gross, flattering or derisive, when a mimic suddenly adopts another human's facial expression or vocal pattern we are amused. Not simply because of their dexterity, nor because of the exaggeration, but because they manage, using a shorthand, to generate vividly in our minds a specific human being, or a cultural trait, or an emotion. And we love the cheat, the obvious cutting of corners to create the illusion.

Dehumanisation

Caricature is not simply a question of exaggeration, nor of shorthand. It also has at its heart the removal of inner causes for behaviour.

Caricature is a display of outward facets of behaviour, without the accompanying inner processes that would normally give rise to them.

When behaviour is dislocated from inner cause, when it is manufactured for its own sake without regard to the inner impulses that would normally generate it, we remove, in a sense, the 'soul'* from the human, leaving a grotesque, outward shell of mannerisms and grimaces. This can be hysterical. It is frightening to see how easily our own behaviour can be dehumanised.

Caricature may also remind us of when we were small, artificially trying it out, aping the adults as we were learning behaviour. I remember at about the age of five, in Switzerland, standing with my hands in my pockets, rocking on the balls of my feet, as my foster-father was wont to do. I have seen little girls adopt a mother's long-suffering look when she can't get her own way. When we laugh at a caricature it may well be that we recognise the soft underbelly of childhood, as we are reminded of the origins of our own behaviour.

Bigotry

So long as caricature is directed towards ourselves it is benign, indeed constructive. So long as we send up our own characteristics, play on our own vulnerabilities and weaknesses, we are making a universal statement about the frailty and pomposity of being human — and laughing at it.

The moment we direct caricature towards a group that is distinctly 'other' than us we do something quite different. We unite our group against *them*. The 'other' might be people of a different race or class. Here is the worst aspect of the unification of the clan. All racist and bigot humour is based on our fear of the stranger in our midst, our discomfort with the unknown. If the face is of a different colour or has different shaped eyes, then it makes it harder for us to understand the subtle facial cues. These cues and our language are the most powerful windows into another person's

---

* There is no religious connotation intended here. I am referring to the composite of all the little factors that make up the deepest elements of our being. A 'spiritual' interaction with the audience is one which has a harmony with them, a connectedness which is so total that it feels religious. We have no better words in the English language as yet to describe such microscopic and yet powerful entities.

soul. If that communication is blurred then so is our view of their soul, and they become less human. If you only understand one language on earth then yours is the proper one and all others are gibberish. Unless we have become familiar with people who are physically disabled we will also see their humanity as diminished, simply because its container is distorted.

When a member of the minority group sends himself up then the picture is entirely different. In Australia at the time of writing we have an extremely popular comedian who has cerebral palsy. Steady Eddie, as he calls himself, says things like, 'I saw a beautiful girl walking down the street yesterday and she smiled at me and I thought to myself — Oh, if only she had a limp.' There is a glow of recognition when we laugh, which tells us that the person who made us laugh knows about things deep inside us. They understand our own vulnerabilities. This elicits in us a sense of, almost, kinship towards them. In sending himself up, Steady Eddie is doing more good for our understanding and acceptance of disabled people than the past 50 years of tentative, pious preaching.

COMEDY 'STYLE'?

I would dearly love to say that there is no such thing as a 'comedy style', that there is no such thing as 'funny acting'. That if you play a scene totally believably, with faith and commitment, and if the situation and the lines are funny, then the performance will also be funny. W. C. Fields, Mae West, Charles Chaplin, Buster Keaton and Peter Sellers have given that illusion for years. But I am afraid we cannot get away from it — there are deep, if subtle, differences between the behaviour of drama and comedy.

1. Naked or Exaggerated Responses

As with caricature, much of comedy contains exaggeration of behaviour. But it need not be as obvious as face pulling. It might be only sensed as a subtle edge of over-seriousness, a moment of deliberation more stunned, a moment of indignation more emphatic, the anger more bared, or the pain more howling.

In real life human beings tend to edit their behaviour in order to not look idiotic, childish, weak. Comedy often allows it to 'all hang out'. Jerry Lewis and Lou Costello gave us pure, unadulterated childhood. Their responses were naked. They did what we are never allowed to do in real life and we loved them for it. Buster Keaton, on the other hand, exaggerated life by letting his face show absolutely nothing.

2. Shallower Feelings

People in comedy tend to recover from emotional states just a smidgen too readily. In real life having a brick drop on your foot leaves a long, lingering pain for many minutes. This after-glow is rarely evident in comedy.

Yosemite Sam in the Bugs Bunny Show is flattened by the drawbridge falling on him. He rattles around as a flattened disk for a while and then pops back to his normal shape. This impossible recovery is what constantly happens to people's emotions in comedy. It is worth noting that a child also can be totally distraught, wailing with grief, be handed an ice-cream and switch straight back to normal. In comedy this quicker recovery is very important. It gives the impression that the pain is not deep-felt. It reminds us that the behaviour is symbolic. The character may have suffered, but not the actor. And so we are given licence to laugh.

3. Contradiction

Comedy often contains two elements of behaviour which seem totally contradictory. Charles Chaplin in *The Gold Rush* is starving and is eating a boiled boot, with the delicacy appropriate to dining in a five star restaurant.

Lou Costello is having something explained to him. He is totally confused, but wears his frown of serious wisdom. Or, he is running along a railway track in front of a train bearing down on him — and he is holding onto his hat! Why is the hat important when you are about to be hit by a train? But again we see the concurrent presentation of two totally different parts of the brain. We have the contrast between life and death desperation, and the niceties of not losing your hat. Notice that the juxtaposition is often between what one is feeling and what one is showing. No doubt much of this has to do with ridiculing our fragile outward covers.

TRUTH IS BEST

Having begrudgingly acknowledged that there is a comic representation of behaviour I now want to back-track. My favourite comic performers on film are Leslie Nielsen (see *The Naked Gun*), Michael Caine (*Without a Clue*), Peter Sellers (*The Pink Panther*) and Gene Wilder (*The Producers*). They give the illusion of playing as straight as possible.

Indeed, the comic considerations should come very late in the development of a performance. The first step is to really understand the dramatic situation. The humour will then arise out of the truth of the moment. If the funny business is there for any other reason, it will either not work, or be irrelevant. Having found the dramatic truth you can now explore ways in which to oppose the obvious, to twist it, enrich it. And finally, every funny little touch will have to be played at precisely the right moment.

3

TIMING

Timing is knowing when the audience is ready for the next piece of information.

This notion is made up of two distinct, and interrelated components. The first, which I call 'inner timing', is the amount of time that it takes for a moment to develop on stage; for example the time it takes for an emotion or thought to develop inside a character, or how long it takes for an interaction to occur between two characters. The second component, which I call 'outer timing', is how long it takes for the audience to perceive that event.

INNER TIMING

Clap your hands. One single, solid clap. Notice how long it takes for the brain to make you aware of the sting, and then how long for the sting to reach its peak and then decay. This is the essence of all timing. How long does it take for an external stimulus to be received; how long for a thought to form; or for an emotion to well up?

OUTER TIMING

This relates to the audience. It is the sense in which we normally use the word 'timing'. When a piece of information is presented to the audience, it takes a certain amount of time for that notion to be perceived, understood and considered. Good timing is knowing at precisely which point of that sequence the next moment should be introduced. There is no such set point. It varies from dramatic moment to dramatic moment, from joke to joke, and these in turn vary from audience to audience.

'Timing' is then made up of three considerations:

1. How fast does the moment develop in the character?
2. At what rate is the audience becoming aware of it?
3. At what stage in their understanding of it must the next piece of information be introduced?

If you are a drama student don't panic, don't throw up your hands, and don't despair. These levels of awareness come with time and application. All that needs to be realised at this stage is that:

1. Every moment of behaviour that you play on stage is a piece

of information being sent to the audience (see Chapter 4).

2. You know what the next piece of information that you're about to send is — the audience doesn't.

3. When exactly you decide to send that piece of information is up to you. This last point is the essence of timing.

Let me repeat.

The fundamental control the performer has over the audience is that she knows what the next moment is, and she can decide when to introduce it.

Jack Benny was considered the comic's comic. His stage persona was that of a mean man. Invariably during the sketch someone would ask him 'Jack, would you lend me $10?' He would put one hand to his face, resting his elbow on the other hand, and do his tired, self-righteous look to the audience. The longer he held the look the more the audience laughed in anticipation. They knew he was going to say 'no'. What they did not know was exactly when. Nor how.

The knowledge of when to bring in the next moment is, in one sense, yours from a very young age. Yet it takes years of practice to refine. At a party you will know the instant that the person you are talking to becomes bored. This needs no training. What to do about it, does.

THE AUDIENCE

When we talk about how long it takes for the 'audience' to become aware of a particular notion, what do we mean? Who is this 'audience'?

It is something less than flattering to be regarded as a member of a semi-predictable human mass, which can be manipulated with some degree of accuracy. After all we are all individuals. We come from different backgrounds, we have different temperaments, different levels of education, different interests. And yet when a hard-won goal is achieved 80,000 people may roar as one. And at the end of an opera 2000 people may rise to their feet. These are unified, gut responses. It seems that we are far more different culturally than we are emotionally. We all have dreams and memories, pains and frustrations. We have all been children.

As each moment of a play is presented to the audience there is a generalised average reception of that piece of information. If it is a comic moment an instantaneous vote is taken. Is this funny? Will I laugh? Are others around me laughing? Not everyone will laugh. Nor will each individual cry at the sad moments. But there *is* an average time taken for the majority of a group of people to receive information and to process it. There is a characteristic emotional make-up to every audience. And it is this entity, this instantaneous vote, this 'soul' of the audience, that one becomes aware of and learns to address, to affect and to manipulate as a performer. Strangely enough it does not reduce individuality, it secretly reinforces it, anonymously, in the dark privacy of a like-minded crowd.

Further, this collective soul reinforces itself. It becomes more homogeneous and united. When a mass of people explodes into laughter it is a very powerful thing. The strays, those who were too fast and saw the joke early, the slow ones who weren't quite there yet, and those for whom the joke is not all that relevant, they will all to some extent be dragged along, by osmosis almost, to share in this united moment of joy. These moments of unification progressively 'tune' the audience in, to be more united in their subsequent responses.

OVER-TIMING & UNDER-TIMING

Timing in both comedy and drama is concerned with how long a gap is needed between consecutive moments of information. Let us go back to the joke model. A joke juxtaposes two distant points on our mental map of the world and asks us to link them. Quickly, suddenly.

> *It is at the instant that a person has first formed a clear notion of the set-up that they are most vulnerable to the punchline.*

If you were telling the joke to one person this is the moment you would wait for before pulling the tag. (This is the knowledge you are almost born with. You can sense the split second that the other person has received the information.) For a group of people in a theatre the time to deliver the tag-line then is when the *majority* of the audience has arrived at this point. When they are facing in the direction indicated by the set-up.

OVER-TIMING

Is waiting beyond that critical moment; by which time minds have accepted the set-up and drifted on. They are beginning to explore new avenues. Waiting that instant too long weakens the sharp juxtaposition between set-up and tag. The momentary confusion will be diluted, as will the associated tension, as will the laugh.

Viewed collectively the majority of the members of the audience will no longer be facing in the direction of the set-up. They will now be pointing every which way and there will be no single direction from which to snap them.

Under-Timing

Is delivering the tag-line before they have understood the set-up, before the majority has arrived at the critical point. If you give the tag-line before they have understood the set-up there can be no switch, no surprise, no joke.

Here is a nice image.

The set-up aims to get the audience onto the rug.

The tag aims to pull the rug out from under them.

In *over-timing* you are pulling the rug after they've wandered off it.

In *under-timing* you are pulling the rug before they've got onto it.

THE MAGIC

If we subscribe to the idea that theatre is magic we must deal with the question: how do we create that magic?

Members of the audience in the foyer before the show will be chatting with their friends and making little jokes. They may have left their children with the babysitter and tipped the cab driver. They may have had dinner and are getting ready to take in a bit of culture. Whatever they have heard about the show they have now come to see for themselves. In our society a theatre audience will be made up of a very wide range of the social spectrum, but it will lean towards professionals, students, academics and business people. They will tend to be reasonably sophisticated, some in very responsible positions. These people have elaborate defence mechanisms; they are worldly; they are in control of their lives.

Yet if we do our job well, within half an hour they will be sitting wide eyed on the edges of their seats — they may be howling with laughter or quietly sobbing in the dark. This is not the behaviour of mature adults. These are children.

When the spell is cast, when the audience is swept away by the illusion, we have touched the child: the imaginative, the sensitive, the defenceless, the uninhibited part of our being. Further, I don't believe that the impact of a play works at the intellectual level.

However sophisticated the thoughts of the play, however beautiful the poetry, however valid the moral arguments, it is only *by touching the child in the members of the audience, that they will be truly affected.*

The design of the set, the costumes, the tricks with light and

TIMING

sound all help to support the magic. But these won't sustain it for two hours. If the play is about people then it is their interactions that will finally be central to the magic. Here is a proposition.

MOMENT BY MOMENT CONTROL

As adults, in every-day life, we control the information coming into us. We edit, select, filter, interpret events as they happen and give them an acceptable coherence. As they occur we judge them and assess them, we file them away or respond to them as appropriately as necessary. In other words to the extent that we control the information coming into us from the outside world, we control that world.

Now imagine that a performer presents the audience with a piece of information, and as soon as they have received it he presents them with the next piece of information, and then the next, and then the next. He never gives the audience time to analyse the bits of information, only to experience them, to take them in. In so doing the actor is asking the members of the audience to enter into a contract with him, to allow him to monitor the information coming into them without them being able to first screen it. In so doing he is asking them to trust him to take them on a journey in which they are not allowed to evaluate — where they only have time to receive and feel. If they agree to this contract then they in fact abrogate their responsibility as adults to control the next couple of hours of their lives. They transfer that responsibility to the artists on the stage. In so doing they lower their defences and become childlike — trusting and dependent; vulnerable, spontaneous, instinctive, innocent, believing.

I call this principle, of constantly providing new moments at the correct rate, the *Moment By Moment* control. It is the mechanism by which we reach the child. It takes some reassurance, some charming to coax a hard-bitten, sophisticated audience into such a contract. And it is then by no means written in stone. The audience can drop out of it at any instant if what the performer is doing is implausible, mis-timed or rings false. The contract is an act of trust from the audience and must be constantly earned. But as the performers build up their credibility the audience will respond with surprising faith and generosity, and once that child has been unleashed the magic becomes palpable.

Vacant Moments

There are times when it is necessary for the audience not to be given any information at all. When we *want* them to consider alternatives, or to re-assess what has just occurred, or to allow a moment to linger. An empty moment can be a very positive thing when intended. It often coincides with a moment where a character has been stunned, or is undecided, or is trying to deal with a new thought or with an emotion welling up.

The Audience Still Thinks

It is an exaggeration to say the members of the audience are not given time to think. As they watch they will all have a little corner of their minds on the overview, on the themes of the piece, on the way it has all been put together. This is as it should be. They will also have flickers of thought about the babysitter, what kind of perfume is sitting next to them or the uncomfortable seats. But in good theatre these thoughts are kept subdued by the deftness and variety of the moments presented.

How Long is a Moment?

A moment is however long it takes for the next emotion to build or for the next notion to form. *There is no such thing as a long pause while the audience is with you. A long pause is any split second that you've lost them.* They will stay with you if they can see that what you are doing is justified — and if you have proven to them at previous moments in the show that when you have paused it has been for a very good reason, that during the pause something has always happened, that out of it has come something worthwhile, something vital. You cannot abuse their trust this time and expect them to stay with you the next time. Nor can you ever let them catch up to you or let them get ahead of you. Because then they become bored, and when a performer plays to a bored audience a little bit of his soul dies. Trust me.

IS COMEDY HARDER THAN DRAMA?

With comedy the accuracy of the timing is obvious. The audience either laughs, or it doesn't. When it doesn't, the jokes appear cruel, silly and ugly. Because that is what all jokes are when they don't work. A comedy without laughs is generally in big trouble. The timing indicators in drama are far more subtle. They are whether we did have a little jump in our seat at that surprise, or whether the hair on the back of our necks did stand up, whether adrenalin did start pumping at that moment and whether we did have a little weep. If the drama were accurately told these things would happen. But a drama can survive without these responses because of its storyline. What it won't be, however, is riveting. The fact is that only mediocre drama is easier to play than comedy. Good drama is every bit as difficult to time as good comedy.

TOTAL THEATRICAL COMMUNICATION

Young actors and directors coming into the industry will often look around at the tired, ineffectual theatre that is ever present and they will quite rightly be driven to search for new, more vibrant forms of expression. They will try anything. In an attempt to achieve vibrancy a director may have performers pretending to urinate or vomit on the stage, or they will have actors go out into the auditorium and abuse the patrons. What they are really looking for is deep, hard, exciting organic interaction between performer and audience. You don't need to urinate. You only need the commitment that it takes from the performer to deal with the audience *Moment By Moment*.

4
ACTING

Few people have been brain surgeons, bus drivers or architects. Only brain surgeons, bus drivers and architects have. But everyone has been an actor. Everyone has learnt to walk and talk by watching others and imitating. Everyone has learnt to adopt the subtle accents, inflections and expressions of their own language. Everyone has had their moment of hogging the floor, with just one more chorus of 'Twinkle Twinkle Little Star' before being sent off to bed. We have all inhabited imaginary worlds as princesses and cowboys. Our fascination with show business therefore is not just hero worship of the stars nor our involvement with the film; it is the fact that at the very heart of our existence we have actually been there, playing out our roles, long ago.

Looking from a much broader perspective we find imitation and pretence proliferating through every form of life imaginable. The miracle of camouflage from stick insect to leopard; the pretence of a kitten learning to stalk and kill a dead leaf — for practice; the bluff of two dogs meeting, standing very close after sniffing, rigid and looking nonchalantly into the distance. The human race did not invent pretence, illusion and imitation. These have existed as long as life itself.

When we come to try to give representations of our own behaviour, however, there seems to be a problem. When you are asked to learn a piece of behaviour, by repeating it over and over what tends to happen is that you end up repeating the form, that is the gestures, the facial expressions, the intonations. It looks fake, manufactured. To reproduce the simple moments of life that the behaviour was meant to represent is clearly elusive.

OLD STYLE/NEW STYLE OF ACTING

Traditionally actors learnt vocal and physical skills that enabled them to precisely repeat the *form* of a performance. The old style laid great emphasis on declamation and gesture, as Hamlet himself warns against to the visiting players. There was an accepted code of communication between performer and audience, a particular pose signified a certain emotion, a facial contortion meant anger. The members of the audience knew that the actor was not angry but they had been trained to translate and accept the symbolic for the real. It was their contribution to the show to immerse themselves imaginatively into the spirit of the presentation. And, as happens with reading and listening to radio, where a large demand is made on the audience's imagination, the old symbolic acting could be extremely moving; so long as it was never seen alongside a realistic representation. With the advent of film, however, where a performance did not need to be repeated hundreds of times, and where tiny facial cues were magnified a hundred-fold, a whole new requirement was born. It happened to coincide with the advent of modern psychology.

Suddenly the 'ham' was obsolete. New representations were needed: realism, interactions that looked organic. That is not to say that everything had to be naturalistic — devoid of style. It simply meant that whatever the style of the piece the characters had to seem to be genuinely interacting with their surroundings rather than indulging us with the theatrical convention itself. The form had to become subservient to the life of the story. The French mime artist, Marcel Marceau, the Bugs Bunny cartoons, Charles Chaplin, Mae West and Laurence Olivier all had this in common. While they each presented behaviour in highly stylised forms, the form itself was never the centre of attention. It simply seemed to exist as part of the extraordinary world in which their characters lived. The form was executed effortlessly, and the rhythms of communication did not contravene what we recognise as simple street honesty.

THE JOB OF THE ACTOR

I have heard it said that acting is not a creative art — it is interpretive. The actor only interprets the lines. For years I have wrestled with this notion. Something seems wrong. True, the writer creates the play. The director conceives it and peoples it with the cast that she chooses. The set, costume, lighting and sound designers all have their input. They can provide the backdrop to this fairyland, and the occasional stunning effect. But they do not provide the constant flow of what the audience 'feels'.

That is the contribution of the actor. It is in creating the spark of life. There, in front of the audience, on the split second, it is she who must breathe life into the moment and touch the audience. By a series of thousands of such moments she will take the audience through the journey of the play and bring that world to life. I can think of no better aim than this: *The job of the actor is to take the dream of the writer and put it into the hearts and minds of the audience.*

WHAT IS BEHAVIOUR?

If we are not to think of pulling faces and giving intonations what are we to do? What is behaviour?

I like J. Z. Young's premise in *Introduction to the Study of Man*. Our fundamental aim on the planet is to survive. We have to find ways to make a living, to protect ourselves and arrange a life that we find palatable. We need to eat. We need shelter and companionship. We require an acceptable status within our group, and a minimum amount of peace of mind. We need sex, warmth, stimulation and security; as well as the gratification of a few other needs — spiritual, aesthetic and philosophical. In other words we also need to have some acceptable view of the world, and of our place in it.

I like to think of the fundamental biological principle homoeostasis: *an organism survives in spite of continual interchange with its surroundings.* The world impacts on us from outside, we have our internal needs driving us from the inside, and we try to balance the two. To survive we interact with the world around us. We deal with it, we do things to it. Behaviour is doing.

Following is a brief introduction to the elements that make up a very powerful model for describing human behaviour, both for acting and for real life.

THE ELEMENTS OF BEHAVIOUR AND ACTING

ACTIONS

The fundamental entity of all behaviour is *the action*. What humans consciously do when they live is — *they play actions*.

> A mosquito lands on your arm and starts sucking. You try to slap it. That is an action.
>
> You have exams coming up and you are studying. That is an action.
>
> A tourist has asked you for directions in the street. You explain to him where he needs to go. That is an action.
>
> An action is any one of the thousands of things we do every day and which make up our *conscious* behaviour. Specifically, actions

are deliberate. Doodling unconsciously while talking on the phone is not an action, but doing a sketch of a vase is. To absentmindedly brush away a fly while reading a book is not an action. To try to catch it is. We will talk about unconscious behaviour presently.

Actions Alter the World

There is an aspect of conscious behaviour which I found far from self-evident when I was first introduced to it: that every deliberate action we perform tries to *alter* something in the world around us. The principle is obvious when the action is to make the bed, for example. At first the bed was a mess, and after you finished the bed was neat and tidy. You effected a change. In the examples above the results would be a squashed mosquito; your brain with new or clearer information; a tourist who knew where he was going.

There are many conscious activities, however, which do not seem to try to alter anything: looking at the night sky, listening to music, lying in the sun, chatting about nothing to a friend. We will return to these in Chapter 5. For the time being it may suffice to say that what these activities affect is your state of mind, your inner being. Taking these subtle examples into account, what we need to understand is that:

1. *An action is any conscious, deliberate act.*
2. *Every action tries to affect something, tries to change something in the world around us (or in the world inside us).*

OBJECTS OF ACTIONS

The thing we are trying to change is called *the object of the action.* (The mosquito, your own brain, the tourist.) The object is what we pay most attention to in real life. Because, *the success or failure of an action is determined by the state of the object after you have played the action.*

As you are making the bed it is the state of the bed which will tell you whether or not you are finished. It is the expression of the tourist which will tell you whether or not he has understood the directions. Conscious behaviour is then *playing actions on objects.* When applied to acting this gets our attention off ourselves, off our voices and off our expressions and gestures. More importantly it is the performer's involvement with the objects of his actions which will make him appear like a living entity, like a character interacting with his surroundings.

George Burns made a beautiful crack after winning the Academy Award for *The Sunshine Boys.* He told BBC's Michael Parkinson, 'Acting's easy. You knock on a door. A man says "Come in". If you come in you're a good actor. If you don't come in you're a bad actor.'

MOTIVATION

Your *reason* for wanting to affect these objects is called your *Motivation*. The mosquito was hurting you; if you fail the exam this time you're out of the course; the tourist seemed like a nice old man and you've been lost yourself at times. When acting, your character's motivation at any moment depends simply on a clear understanding of the story. Why is he or she doing this at this moment? When the actor is not clear about the inner life of his character he has very little chance of communicating anything meaningful to the audience. Working out a rough understanding of the motivations involved seems to me to be simple politeness to the audience; a prerequisite to any kind of performance.

THE REFERENCE

When acting, as well as the character's *Motivation* in the story, there will come a time when the actor needs her own personal motivation to create the moment. In my drama school that was called the actor's *Reference* (Chapter 6). After a certain number of takes on film or on television, or after a few weeks in a stage play, it will no longer be possible to simply believe the story and come up with the appropriate feelings. A reference is then a thought that the actor can conjure up in order to help her feel what the character is supposed to be feeling at that moment. References are parallel, personal thoughts that flit through the actor's mind throughout the performance. They are made up of a patchwork of memories, imaginings and delusions. One might be the memory of a real incident, another the memory of a moment in a book or a film. Often it might simply be the silent thought of what the character might actually be thinking. If I say to you 'Eiffel Tower' an image of that beautiful structure will momentarily flash through your mind. The process of triggering that image is what we are talking about; it is as simple as that.

A reference is a very personal thing. Your response to the idea of 'a snake' may be quite different to that of someone who had pet snakes as a child. Nevertheless, each person has their particular associations, and millions of memories to draw from.

THE COLOUR OF THE ACTION

The feeling with which you play an action is called the *Colour*. Sadly, happily, suspiciously. With very few exceptions, both in real life and in acting, we do not strive to create the colour directly. It is never what we think about. It is a by-product of the action being played and what the character is thinking. It is the end result of the references you are touching within yourself.

I saw a lady in a dreadful fifties movie (*Juke Box Rhythm*), pulling faces, 'showing' her emotions, presenting attitudes: the guarded question, consternation, grief. She was imposing her feelings directly onto the face and the voice. And it occurred to me that it was like trying to make a flower grow by pulling it up by the stem. That's not the way. You feed it and water it, from below. Then it will grow. Imposing the emotion onto the face directly in this way, we call 'playing the colours' (as opposed to playing the actions).

There are instances when we do put on fake emotions, such as when a child has hurt itself slightly and we pout in sympathy, and say silly things like, 'Oh, the poor little finger. Nasty, nasty door!'

ADJUSTMENTS

An enormous part of our behaviour is in fact unconscious. The Italian man does not try to speak in an Italian accent any more than you try to write in your own handwriting. These are not deliberate aspects of behaviour, they do not try to affect anything. We call them *Adjustments*.

Adjustments are those aspects of behaviour to which we pay little or no attention in real life.

Consider the activity of driving. If you are experienced the things that will occupy your mind are whether or not to let another car into your lane; whether it is this street or the next that you have to turn right into, and then to make sure that the way is clear when you do make the turn. These are all examples of actions, the conscious things you do. On the other hand you will rarely think about pressing the accelerator or the brake, or switching on the indicator. You are even less conscious of how you move your hand in going from the radio to the steering wheel, or how you hold your head when looking into the rear-vision mirror. These are adjustments. They are automatic. Habitual. We do not think about them.

Whether an activity is an action or an adjustment depends on how much attention you pay to it.

While your attention is on the road and on the surrounding traffic, changing gears is an adjustment. If the gear stick won't engage, however, and you have to momentarily look down and push it in, then changing gears has become an action. Being aware of where you are directing your attention at any moment, the understanding of which part of your behaviour is action and which is adjustment, has extremely important ramifications for acting. We will address these in Chapter 7.

In every day life the way you walk, the dialect of English in which you speak, the timbre of your voice, your mannerisms and idiosyncrasies, any limps, tics or lisps; these are all adjustments.

Altering their adjustments is one of the main ways that actors disguise themselves. Limps and accents and exotic mannerisms are what so many people regard as 'real' acting — if you can change yourself into a very old man, or better still, into a woman, then you must be okay. Many actors are good natural mimics. If you are a good mimic then you will be good at adjustments.

Because so little attention is paid to our adjustments in real life, it is precisely the practising of new adjustments that takes up most of the time when preparing for a role. Endless drill is required to make new habits become automatic. We call this 'the working-in of the adjustments'. The most common of course is learning one's lines. But it might also mean acquiring a different accent, or learning to mime playing an instrument to a set piece of music, or nimbly handling a tennis racquet when you don't in fact play.

Type Casting

You need very little work on adjustments when the character you are playing has the same general demeanour, attributes, background and skills as yourself. When you have been type cast there are only two set of adjustments you will need to work-in. Learning what to say, and where to move. (See Mitchum's quote, page 81.)

Voice and Body

As an actor your voice and movements are what carry the thought. You have no other channels through which to speak to your audience. In order to be able to clearly convey the subtlest of notions you will need to have good control and flexibility of voice and body. One could say that acquiring these skills are the first examples of the working-in of adjustments.

There are other, more pragmatic reasons however for training the voice and the body. Survival. It takes discipline to play moments of rage every night and twice on matinee days, and still have some shred of a voice left at the end of the month. Likewise physical dexterity is not only an asset for versatility, for funny walks and trembling hands. A slap, a fall or a sudden move may be quite harmless when done occasionally. But when you repeat them over and over at rehearsals, and fly into them in the heat of the performance, it is very easy to get bruised, or to pull a muscle or to tear a tendon if you don't know what you are doing.

Protection of the voice and body also requires meticulous warming up.

The Style of the Performance
The style in which we act in a particular play or film, that is, the handling of the voice, the accent, the movement and bearing of the character, in fact all of the 'form' of the performance falls into this basket — of adjustments. If the lines of Shakespeare are to sound comprehensible and the poetry natural then they must be skilfully worked-in. To look as though one is concerned with mouthing the lines and striking stylish poses we call 'playing the adjustments' (as opposed to playing the actions).

That is not to say that your character cannot be a fop, full of affectations and mannerisms. He can deliberately mouth a word or hold up his little finger when picking up his cup of tea. He is allowed to play arrogant actions on the people around him and now and again to deliberately use his voice and mannerisms in order to top them. But be sure that it is the character who is playing with the mannerisms and not the actor. The first does it as a genuine attempt to deal with the world around him as effectively as he knows how, the second does it to show off his dexterity to the audience. The actor can easily fall into the trap of titillating the audience with a show about funny styles instead of simply telling them a story about a character who happens to live in a flamboyant world.

We will discuss adjustments in more detail in Chapter 7.

THE METHOD APPROACH TO ACTING
This way of looking at the different components of behaviour — Actions, Objects of Actions, Motivations and Adjustments — forms the basis of the so called *Method* approach to acting. It was originated by Konstantin Stanislavsky in Russia at the turn of the century and was disseminated by Lee Strasberg and Stella Adler and others in America in the 1930s and 40s; and it came to me via my own mentor Hayes Gordon, here in Sydney. These notions have found their way into branches of social psychology, such as transactional analysis.

When the approach first appeared, to the old actors the very idea of working out the character's 'motivation' was bad enough. The notion then of the actor's personal 'references' was preposterous. What was the point of delving into all this psychological garbage when really all you had to do was simply say the line, dear boy?

It did not help that the approach was made popular by a clutch of charismatic Hollywood film stars who mumbled, because they tended to play working class heroes. Their performances were revolutionary in their naturalism — they would hesitate and fumble and pause and scratch. I remember an ad in *Honi Soit*, the Sydney University student paper, around 1962, blaring 'Come and see spitting, punching, farting Marlon Brando in *The Wild One*!' This all led to the 'Method' becoming seen as a *style* of acting, rather than an approach. It became regarded as a movement in theatre opposed to discipline, elegance and classical form; when all it had really been intended for was to provide the actor with appropriate little thoughts to enable him to play the moments honestly.

You Can't Keep Believing It

References would not be necessary if we could keep believing in the story indefinitely, and if we were able to spontaneously feel what we were meant to feel at any moment in the play. But anyone who has even done amateur theatre will tell you that that does not happen. Let us toy with the example of Hamlet. You've got the role. The rehearsals progress, the reality of this imaginary world takes shape and by the time you open you can believe that you are him, Prince of Denmark, here at Elsinore Castle and this is Gertrude, your mum, and this is your sword. And it's terrific. Why not? It's like playing cowboys and indians really; you can believe it. For a while. And then, gradually, moments creep in when you know it's not true. That's a wooden floor. This is a stage. Those moments become more frequent, and finally you can only believe that you are acting. Why else are all these people sitting out there watching you? And why are you doing all of this again tonight when you did it all last night and the night before? And this is not your mother. She's an actress. And while she is a very nice lady her lipstick is on crooked again, and she always cuts you off on that bloody line!

When you can no longer believe it, the feelings that your character is meant to have will no longer spontaneously appear. You may try to push and squeeze them out of your soul and you may try to fake them, as did the lady in *Juke Box Rhythm* (page 29). But this will not give you moments of life. Just well-meant histrionics.

Now is the time when you will need the skills, the little thoughts, the sleight of hand to trick yourself.

Here's another George Burns line, 'All you need to be a good actor is to learn to be absolutely sincere. Once you can fake that you're made.'

HOLDING BACK

The following notion is as fundamental to this approach to acting as is the idea that *behaviour is 'doing'*. The notion is this:

We do not try to show our feelings. We try to hold them back.

In real life we would prefer not to be seen as trembling lumps of jelly, buffeted around by the whims of our feelings. We have wonderful defence mechanisms which assure us a certain degree of stability. Whenever a strong emotion hits us these defences instantly push us in the opposite emotional direction, towards equilibrium.

We have all heard of people being told that they had won the lottery who immediately burst into tears. Hours later they had recovered and were revelling and rejoicing and pinching themselves to make sure that it was true. We have also heard of people, having been told of the death of a close relative, stop for a moment, smile, even give a laugh and say incredulously 'What?' Moments later they might walk around saying 'Well! That's that.' Hours later they will have crumpled as the full force of the grief begins to hit.

The point is that we do not instantly give way to our emotions. We resist. We try to maintain equilibrium. Like when being pushed, we do not immediately fall over. We instinctively oppose the force in order to keep our balance. If the force towards happiness is too great and too sudden our trying to maintain equilibrium may send us so far the other way that we cry. When the news is horrendous enough our defences will send us in the opposite direction, into areas of lightness and perhaps even laughter.

I have chosen extreme examples to make the point of the internal ballast. But our defence mechanisms are just as busy in everyday life. We need them to withstand all the little bumps and jostles of social interaction. We don't instantly expose our uncomfortable feelings. We find it hard to acknowledge real gratitude, we try not to nauseate our friends with our own good fortune, nor to drag them into our despair. People who do expose themselves too readily tend to be seen as weird.

There are of course people who do not try to hide their feelings at all. The car salesman will ooze his sincerity. The madman will freely laugh at passers-by, or rail at the elements. The neurotic will grab your arm and weep on your shoulder. These are the exceptions. If you are deliberately trying to show your feelings in real life it is more than likely that you are either lying or mad. That is the joy of playing insane people. You can make every mistake in the acting book and come out looking brilliant. It is very difficult to mess up the role of Ophelia. It is sometimes referred to as actor-proof.

The attempt to maintain emotional equilibrium is beautifully summed up by the statement:

The drunk man tries to walk straight, he does not try to stagger.

And it is precisely by the manner in which we resist showing our emotions, in the way that we deal with the world in spite of them, that the world can see what we feel.

This leads me to the generalisation:

Bad acting is showing the audience what the character is feeling. Good acting is doing what the character would do if he felt that way.

To fight against a feeling we must first generate it. You can't hold back something that isn't there. That is why we need *references*. The process of generating a feeling by thinking an appropriate thought is called 'loading up'.

Loading up an emotion, holding it back and then simply playing the action constitutes for me the Holy Grail of acting.

William Shakespeare gives one of his characters, Claudius, the King in *Hamlet*, a line very relevant to any discussion of references. Claudius has just been praying to God for forgiveness for having killed Hamlet's father (Act III scene 4). At the end he gets off his knees and says bitterly,

> My words fly up, my thoughts remain below:
> Words without thoughts never to heaven go.

Load up Slightly More than you Need
In order to be able to hold back your emotions always load up more than will be visible from the outside. A simple way of saying it is that if you are supposed to appear quietly angry at someone you should be holding back shouting at them. If you have to shout at them have enough loading to want to hit them. If you have to hit them

hold back from killing them. And if you have to kill them hold back from destroying the world. It sounds dramatic but I think that to some extent that does reflect what actually happens in real life.

SUMMARY

The ACTION is *what* we do.

The OBJECT of the action is what we do it *to*.

The MOTIVATION is *why* we do it.

The REFERENCE is the actor's personal reason for doing and his emotional trigger.

The COLOUR is the feeling with which you play an action.

The ADJUSTMENTS are all the unconscious, habitual characteristics and mannerisms of behaviour.

5
PLAYING ACTIONS

In a video on world champion boxer, Mike Tyson, his one-time trainer and manager Gus D'Amato was speaking on building up the will in an athlete as opposed to his skill.

'The coward and the hero they both feel the same — it's what they do that makes them different. In other words the hero feels just as frightened as the coward. But it's just that the coward, he runs, instead the hero he feels the same and he has the discipline. He just makes himself go through whatever has to be done. It's what he does that makes him a hero and what the other fellow doesn't do that makes him a coward.'

We are what we do seems to be D'Amato's message.

To use the word 'action' to refer to physical activities that we perform on the world around us makes everyday sense. To throw a ball, to hammer a nail, to sweep the path and to make the bed are actions, pretty much in the normal sense of the word. When we start to talk about actions in the context of interactions between people then we need to have a closer look at what we mean.

Consider again the tourist asking us directions. How can giving directions be regarded as an action? Because as a result of our communication with him the tourist has undergone a change. Before it he did not know the way. Afterwards he did. What caused the difference was the action that we played on him.

But how did we do this? If we don't think of inflections and intonations, what do we do with words?

THE THOUGHT PACKAGE

'Could you please pass the salt?' can be regarded, not as a group of words with a particular intonation, but as a thought package being sent to the person being addressed. They will receive this package and hopefully respond by passing you the salt. Every time we communicate with someone we can think of it as sending them a thought package. That is in fact what we do when we play an action. The object of the action is the person we are addressing. And the action will try to have some kind of effect on them (in this case to have them pass you the salt). Playing an action then is like throwing a ball. If the speech is long it simply means that there is a whole string of thought packages being sent. But what is vital is that we understand that *each little bundle of intelligence that we send to another person is an action that we play on them,* because it tries to affect them.

NAMES OF ACTIONS

There are millions of different kinds of bundles that we can send to one another, each trying to have a different effect. One can be a reassuring action, another a challenging action, another a 'getting them to admit to something' type of action. So that is what we call them: the action 'to reassure', 'to challenge', 'to get them to admit'. In the Appendix I have listed 200 or so of the more common names that we give to actions to give you a feel for the kinds of ways we can think about human interactions. The idea is to use interesting, evocative names that don't just define the behaviour but stimulate the imagination when it comes to playing them. 'To head the other person off at the pass' is more interesting than 'to try to stop her'. 'To take the wind out of her sails' is better than 'to make her lose confidence'.

It is very difficult at first to give actions names. To observe a person and try to decide what they want to achieve is at first frustrating. You know what they're doing but you can't put it into words. And it is not as simple as saying 'Oh, they just felt like saying that'. That is true of everything, so it tells us nothing. The reason for trying to give these things names is to try to create some kind of order in one's perception of what it is that people do to each other. And it is wonderful practice to sit at a party or in a store and watch people, and try to name the actions that they are playing on each other. When one young lady says to another 'That is a lovely dress you're wearing. I've got a very similar one.' is she approving of her girlfriend's taste or is she showing her that she is more in fashion by having bought hers first?

There is of course only one way to learn to name actions: observe, observe, others, yourself, observe.

Let me add that in the end the names are meant to help, to clarify. If you are stumped when working on a script, but you know exactly what the person is doing to the other, my drama teacher used to say 'I don't care if you call it spinach as long as you do it.' Often if you leave it for a day or two an appropriate phrase will pop into your head.

Guided Missiles

'Come on, where were you last night? — I want to know.'

Here are two sentences. The person speaking asks the question. There is no response, so they persist. We can call the first part the action 'to pin the other person down' and the second part, indeed, 'to persist'. This is a clear example of two little thought packages being sent — two distinct actions being played. (Three if you separate 'Come on' from 'where were you last night?') It is useful to get used to this idea of distinct little bundles of thought or intention or information flying back and forth between humans as we communicate.

If, however, we consider the whole thing as one single action and call the composite bundle, 'to get the other person to open up' then we get the feeling that the combined action is more like a guided missile than, say, a bullet. You try to open them up, they don't, so you keep trying. The guided missile is a very useful notion. In real life you don't just fire an action and close your eyes

and hope that it will hit its mark. As you play it you tend to watch the other person for little responses, for shifts in their attitude; a look away, a long suffering sigh. As they move so you adjust so that your action will impinge on them regardless of where they try to escape to. We call this *following through* with your action. Most actions aim at moving targets.

The Follow Through

To Follow Through is what we call the act of continuing to play the action a moment after we have stopped speaking (whether or not the target is moving). Following through is common practice. We do it to make sure that the action has impinged and to look for the result. We have said 'I want to know.' and then we keep sending the same silent message to the other person for a moment longer.

Incidentally, if we regard the action as a guided missile, then we can regard the object of the action as the target, and the motivation as the fuel.

The Playing of an Action

We humans have very little to say as yet about the actual sending and receiving of the thought packages. What is it exactly that is transmitted by a look or a shrug or a phrase? And how exactly is it received and interpreted? This is fascinating stuff, at the very forefront of scientific thought. But here is a suggestion of one of the mechanisms involved in the doing of it.

When playing an action we momentarily bring to mind a picture of how the other person will look if we succeed in playing the action. We then behave towards them in such a way that we think will make them approach that state.

The Light Bulb

When learning to act I found it useful to think in terms of trying to light up a light bulb above the other person's head. This might have been a bulb of reassurance or intimidation, a bulb of clarification or encouragement, depending on the action that I was playing. But as you played the action on them you were trying to light this specific bulb.

I think that this vision of the aimed-for end result in the other person is the tool that I rely on more than any other at the actual instant of playing the action. I have observed a great many actors do something very similar — following the other person's tiny responses, and manoeuvring them towards a required state as they spoke. This has nothing to do with the Method as such. It seems to be at the very heart of our visual and vocal communication.

AN EXERCISE

As part of our general training we must have spent the better part of two years at the Ensemble Theatre learning this one skill: to play clear, specific actions. We did this primarily through improvisations — scenes whose situation had been prepared but whose dialogue was invented on the spur of the moment. I now regard improvisation as an invaluable technique for teaching acting, as you will see in Chapter 13.

We had a variety of exercises to teach us action play, but the most basic one which I still use with my pupils is this. Two people are each given an action to play. The actions are conflicting, but they only have one each. They prepare an improvisation in which their character will be playing their allotted action. The catch is this. *Each person is only allowed to play their one allotted action and no other throughout the whole course of the improvisation.* Everything they say and do has to belong to that action, in spite of anything that the other person might do or say.

Now this is a totally artificial exercise. We do not in real life keep playing the one single action relentlessly. We twist and turn and adjust our behaviour depending on what we want and how the other person is responding.

Let us say that the two actions were 'to accuse' and 'to get the other person off your back'. You always choose conflicting actions or there would be no scene. (If one person said, 'Let's go outside' and the other said, 'OK', they would just get up and walk out! Consider this. 'Juliet, will you marry me?' 'Oh, yes Romeo!'. They embrace. End of play. For a scene or play to sustain itself it must have conflict. This applies to all drama, to all comedy.)

So, for 'to accuse' and 'to get the other person off your back' the two students might decide that one would be a mother accusing her son of not getting a job, not helping around the house, etc. and the other would be the son. After a few minutes' preparation they would get up and do the improvisation. Now, in a normal situation, during the course of accusing her son, a mother might also play actions like 'to check on what he has just said', 'to challenge', 'to query' or 'to despair'. In this exercise she was only allowed to play 'to accuse'. He, on the other hand is stuck with 'to get her off his back'. He must not play 'to justify', nor 'to get out from

PLAYING ACTIONS

> under', nor 'to confront her in return' — just, 'to get her off his back'.
>
> Artificial as this exercise is, it is very powerful. It gives us a slow-motion opportunity to focus our activities on playing one clear, single action throughout the period of the improvisation. Whatever the other person does to us we are called upon to respond to them, to interact with them, plausibly, proportionally, playing only that one action. The end result is that in the distant future if we are playing a character who has to 'get someone off their back' it will mean something to us. We will have an idea of the lightbulb we are trying to light in the other person. And after two years' practice of these kinds of exercises it does become possible to finally play an action simply, without pulling faces, without putting on attitudes. This particular exercise will also help us be more flexible in taking direction. No matter what the situation, or what the other character has said, we will be able to find a reason for playing a particular action.
>
> What I find remarkable is that the concept of an action is so evocative, so natural to us, that within minutes two students, totally new to this, can get up and do an improvisation from which the majority of the class will be able to guess what actions they were playing.

SELF-CONSCIOUSNESS

When you step out onto a stage and see an ocean of people looking at you, it is almost impossible to not want join them and look at yourself too. The result is disastrous. You cannot move, you cannot speak. Your will is somehow sucked out of you by that huge, black, easily bored mass.

You cannot respond to the actors around you if you are looking at yourself. And if you do look at yourself and you see a trembling, self-conscious person, that will make you even more self-conscious. It is a vicious circle.

A huge bonus of playing actions is that it breaks that cycle, because it forces your attention onto the object of your action — namely the other person. As we have said, in order to play an action you must constantly be aware of the other person's state to guide your next moment. As you do this your self-consciousness decreases which in turn allows you to become freer to interact with the world around you. (When you are alone on stage then the object of your action will be your own thoughts and internal images, and finally the audience. Affecting them and taking them on a journey is quite different from passively submitting to their scrutiny.)

DO NOT PLAY THE ACTION 'TO BE'

One of the central principles of this approach is never to try to play actions such as 'to be happy', or 'to be sad'. Because to do so is to go straight back to where acting was 100 years ago. Players came out and *showed* their feelings. If you try to play the action 'to be happy' that is what you will do. Your aim will be to show us how happy you are. And fake, artificial grins will become plastered all over your face. A constant theme running through this book will be that a better approximation of life is *to generate the appropriate feeling and then fight against it*. We will see how to generate feelings in the next chapter.

Furthermore if you do try to play an action like 'to be happy' *you* will become the object of your action. Because the only way you will be able to tell whether or not you are looking happy is by looking at yourself. And zap! That will lead you straight back to self-consciousness.

This advice is not to be confused with situations where a character bucks themselves up, or chastises themselves. It is perfectly legitimate for one part of you to talk to another part of you. Tennis players scream at themselves for missing a point. That is fine. What they are doing is trying to regain focus. They are playing the action 'to kick themselves in the bum'. They are not playing the action 'to be angry', or even 'to be a better player'. They are kicking themselves.

It is equally dangerous to try to *be* the character. First, if you ever really succeed in believing that you are the character you will end up in the loony bin. Second, it is not necessary; and third, it does not actually work. Because trying to 'be' the character tends to blur your eyes to what the character would actually be seeing and bouncing off. As you are busy trying to *be* you get distracted from actually *doing*.

The main way we have of knowing who someone is is by watching what they *do*. Our every-day street wisdom, our normal sensitivity is often so subtle, so finely tuned that it can tell us about a person's deepest recesses. It follows that if we want to convince people that we are a particular character we simply have to do what they would do. This does work: Do exactly what the character does, think what they think, feel what they feel and you will appear to *be* that character. 'We are what we do' as D'Amato said.

How to do, think and feel as the character is the subject of the next chapter.

SUMMARY

1. An action is a verb, a doing word or phrase.
2. Everything that we do consciously, deliberately in life is an action.
3. Every action tries to achieve something, to alter something in the world around us.

    We can think of an action as a guided missile,

    the object of the action is then the target and

    the motivation is the gun powder or rocket fuel.

    The adjustments would then be the shape and colour of the missile.

6
MOTIVATION

An Australian journalist, Matt White, while working in London in the fifties had a theatre review-cum-showbiz column, which was being read by some fifteen million people. On his return to Australia an interviewer (Frank Crooke) asked him, 'Wasn't that tremendous power? Couldn't you make or break a show? How did you feel writing for all those people?' Matt said, 'If I'd thought about the fifteen million people I wouldn't have been able to write a word. I used to write as though I was telling my Auntie Flo in Australia.'

This is an example of the little mental tricks we use quite naturally to enable us to do things which would have been impossible otherwise. Such a little thought-trick is called 'a reference'.

Here is another example. As a young actor I did some stand-up comedy around the Sydney clubs, on and off for about three years. Hayes Gordon had said to us in class, 'People, you should all do vaudeville, variety, stand-up.' And naive, gullible pupil that I was I took him literally, and it was invaluable. I will return to this later. But when I was starting out if I ever saw a person looking even slightly bored my heart would sink. I immediately imagined that everyone else in that room was feeling just as bored as that man in the third row but they were all too polite to show it. After only a few months however, I started to find myself thinking 'He's playing bored at the moment, he's resisting me. That's OK, he's allowed. He is resisting because nothing I have done so far has hit him hard enough. But this next gag is going to get him, he will love it. He has no idea it's coming and it is going to crack him.' Exactly the same stimulus, a bored face, was now being interpreted in a very different way. It now gave me reason to go on, instead of reason to stop. It just takes a flick of the mind to reinterpret and turn a possible negative into a positive. Twisting the meaning of real things is only one approach. All the different ways of finding references are called *motivational techniques*. They all aim at one simple thing: to nimbly trick your mind into thinking things that will help you play the next moment.

Note that a reference flashes through your mind in a glimmer. It would take you several pages to describe what appeared in your mind when you read the words: Eiffel Tower. But the *time* that it took for those images to be created, and then to fade, is at the heart of all timing. Following is a brief list of the most common mental tricks that we use to delude ourselves.

MOTIVATIONAL TECHNIQUES

I will only discuss a few of these mental sleight of hand here. I simply want to give you a feel for the kinds of machinations that are available. Again they are very personal. I'm sure that we all discover some for ourselves and we each eventually decide on our own favourites.

1. BELIEF IN THE SITUATION

This is the most basic. It needs very little introduction. It is what we all did as children when playing games and day-dreaming. It is the first approach of all acting — simply to believe in who you are, the situation and what your character is doing. If this could be relied on indefinitely we would need nothing else.

2. USURY

This involves taking in the real things happening around you, but twisting their meaning to support you in what you have to do. My story about the bored man in the third row is such an example (page 44). I find this motivational technique more flexible, more versatile and more powerful than any other. I use it almost exclusively, hand in hand with another couple. This is not only because of its vast range of applications, but also because it, more than any other technique, keeps you in total contact with your surroundings. The reason is that any information that comes to you is fair game. Almost anything that the other actor says or does, almost any response from the audience, can be interpreted to help you in your next moment.

Let us say that at some point in the play you are supposed to reassure the other actor. He is supposed to come on looking a little worried, a little insecure and your action is to reassure him. Tonight he walks on looking unusually confident. What do you do? How do you reassure someone who doesn't need it? Why would you? It is not a great stretch of the imagination to believe that he is bluffing; that his inappropriate confidence tonight must be covering some extra fear. Perhaps he has friends in the audience, making him nervous and forcing him to show more bravado than usual? That's probably it! And suddenly he does need your reassurance, and your support.

If Hamlet can no longer believe in the situation, when he has to vehemently confront Gertrude in Act III scene 4, then part of his anger might very well come from the fact that she does tend to cut his lines off at certain points. If this habit of hers does in fact irritate him then he would be a fool not to use it. It will give him a simple, natural loading for playing the scene. I know this sounds a little callous, but good acting in many ways demands a ruthless self-honesty. From inside yourself you cannot afford to be over-polite or squeamish. It is very difficult to act well, and the internal mechanisms cannot afford all the external social graces. Virtually no means can be ignored to achieve a good result. We can comfort ourselves in the knowledge that nobody knows what you are thinking. Not even your fellow actors. All anyone sees is a well justified, spontaneous performance; which is what the audience wants and what your co-workers need. Provided you do what you do with care and consideration for others, I regard any reference that works, totally permissible. And I do mean any.

As regards the audience, usury again is all powerful. Whether someone laughs or coughs or gasps can be interpreted to mean that they are happy, sad, riveted or overcome with emotion. The only limits are your own abilities of self-delusion and imagination. Mind you, according to Sir Ralph Richardson, a good performance was one 'which kept the audience from coughing'.

3. THE LIGHT BULB
We have already met the light bulb in Chapter 5, but for me it turns out not only to be merely a description of what automatically happens when you play an action; it also becomes its own reason for doing. As I try to light a particular bulb in the other person, and as I see that it is not yet quite lit, I am driven to continue. For example, I start to play the action to clarify, like when giving the tourist directions. So long as I see he doesn't yet fully understand where he has to go I have good reason to continue playing the action. Trying to light that light bulb becomes its own motivation.

4. AS IF
With 'as if' you embellish the scene with an imaginary condition. For example, you have a scene in which you are waiting for a job interview. Once the initial belief has worn thin, it might help you to think that this is a little bit as if you were waiting to see the dentist. Then again depending on your own background and the requirements of the scene, you might need to think that this was as if you were psyching yourself up for a race.

Here is a more elaborate example. Let us say that you are one of the people hiding in the attic in the play *The Diary of Anne Frank*. You can hear the German soldiers downstairs, and you are terrified that they are about to burst through the door. The problem is that by this stage of the season you know the actors playing the soldiers so well, with all their idiosyncrasies and senses of humour, that it is very difficult to be frightened by them. I would ignore all the noise and the military stomping, which is only there to build the tension for the audience. Instead, see if you can imagine that in amongst all those fake theatrical sounds you can hear the gentle padding of a fully grown lion. He has escaped, he is on the loose and he is here in this house. Interpret any particularly obtrusive noise as a soft growl, or take it that the lion has knocked something over, to allow your responses to remain proportional to what the audience is hearing. He is hungry, he is sniffing around and if you breathe he will hear you. I think, for a while, this would work for me.

If you can believe it, it forces you to focus on something outside of yourself, it forces you to listen, it imposes conditions on your breathing and on your very metabolism, which is in keeping with the extreme fear of the character in the scene.

5. Just Like

This is very similar to 'as if' but instead of substituting for the situation you substitute for the character you are speaking to. For example you might think, 'This is just like talking to my grandmother when I was little.' Matt White's writing for his Auntie Flo is a wonderful example (page 44). When doing a one-person show and having to respond to imaginary people, this can be very useful. It enables you to particularise the other person's reactions and their attitudes, thereby giving your own responses to them a plausibility and life. It can also help in preparing for a scene. Before going on stage think that the way your character feels towards the person you are about to meet is very similar to the way you felt towards your dad before that final confrontation just before you left home.

However, when it comes to playing a scene with another actor I give this technique a wide berth. It does not work for me to look at someone and try to imagine that they are someone else. It blinds me to parts of what they are actually doing, which means that I am missing out on valuable information. I find usury far more effective because it takes in the whole person, as they are, warts and all. It could be that my skills with 'just like' are limited because I so rarely use it, but whenever I have tried I always found that it cut me off from the other actor, because the imagined person got in the way.

6. Sense Memory

Sense Memory is an all-purpose assistant to any technique you are likely to use. It is the experiencing of real sensations by simply imagining the stimulus. Please allow yourselves comfortable pauses between them as you read the next few phrases.

> Imagine the sound of your local church bells.
> The sound of the birds in the morning.
> Imagine the smell of cut grass.
> The smell of an Italian coffee shop.
> The smell of an orange.
> The feel of your quilt, your bedding.

If you had a glimmer of a sensation in any of those then you experienced a 'sense memory'. It is not a technique which lives on

MOTIVATION 49

its own, but it is invaluable in bringing thousands of little moments to life. It provides colour and texture to a performance in a way that no other technique can because it generates flashes of real experiences.

The example of listening for the lion involves 'sense memory'.

It is particularly useful in film, where by the time they come to film your close-up in the coffee shop (at the very, very end of the day), anything that will not actually appear on camera is likely to be cleared from the set. So not only will the coffee have gone but so will the actor that you are meant to be talking to. The sense memory smell of the coffee will help you. So will a powerful 'just like' to help you do your lines to the first assistant.

(I loathe playing with definitions. Forgive me. I am labelling terms here as an introduction, for clarity. Generally definitions are only useful when things go wrong. Then it really does help to have very clear concepts with which to analyse what is happening, in order to correct the problem. In all other instances precise definitions in art are far more important to its dissectors than to its creators.)

7. Emotion Memory

This is the most dangerous and controversial of all the techniques. Please treat this one with great respect. I am not being sensational. If you are in any way emotionally unstable, if you feel vulnerable or susceptible to big emotional swings please do not try it. Even if you think that you are perfectly fit I would advise that you only explore this one in the presence of a qualified drama tutor.

This technique alters your mood. It will produce an emotional change which will last for several minutes. If the reference you pick is particularly strong and you do not know how to turn it off the mood may linger for hours. Consequently, it is very useful as a means for preparing for a scene when you want a particular feeling to affect you throughout the scene. At first I do not recommend that you try to use it within a scene because, as you will see, it also tends to cut you off from your surroundings. With experience, however, you will be able to flash an image in your mind which will have precisely the deep, emotional effect on you that the character requires at that moment.

Here is how you learn it. You decide on the emotion you want to generate; we'll play safe and start with happiness. You sit down on a chair, close your eyes, and pick some moment in your life which made you very happy. If you can find some instance when you were around five or eight, an early, vulnerable, age all the better. But truly, any clear, sharp moment when something occurred which suddenly brought on a burst of happiness will do. Any wonderful news which gave you something that you had deeply wanted. Having decided on such a moment in your life do not try to recreate how you *felt*.

Your eyes are closed and you simply remember where you were when you got the news, or when the event happened. Were you indoors or outside? If you were inside think of the room you were in. What did it smell like? Where were you in the room? Where was the light coming from? Were there windows? What sort of curtains? What kind of flooring? Carpet? What sort of pattern? What were you doing? Who else was there? What were they wearing? What were their expressions? How did you discover the wonderful information? Who said it? How did they look?

By now you will be starting to feel some of that deep warm glow that came over you during that experience, not by trying to recapture it directly, but by simply recalling all the other details of the event. The same process applies for sadness and grief. You just pick an event which was for some reason very painful. You can see that this process could be disturbing. In class I will tend to take a student through the sad one first, allow the class to observe the change, and then immediately talk them through the happy one. That way the final after-glow is pleasant.

If you ask the pupil to tell you what they had for dinner last night before the beginning of the exercise, and ask them to tell you that again after taking them through the sad emotion memory, you will have a yardstick of behaviour to go by. Their subtle responses, the amount of cover-up and hold back, will be so apparent. Ask them again after taking them through the happy emotion memory and you will again see a whole new behaviour; freer, lighter, more spontaneous.

I see this whole exercise more as a means of learning, than as a technique for acting. It enables you to learn to generate deep emotions at will. It takes a cumbersome route to do it, but it does slowly take you on a journey which, with experience, you will be able to cover in an instant. Also with experience you will not remain glued to high emotional moments of your own life, but you may simply think of a scene in a film which always makes you sad, or makes you laugh, or you may think of a photo which triggers something very deep in you. Our natural defence mechanisms do not allow us to immediately access deep emotions. We can think the thought but the emotion will instantly slip away as we protect ourselves from discomfort. As I say, I see this exercise as a means of initially oiling the wheels. It allows us to get used to exposing ourselves to these emotions, so that we may eventually be able to tap and easily respond to the more powerful references locked away deep inside us.

8. Miscellaneous

Having mentioned some of the most famous techniques we are now left with the infinity of other little tricks that actors use. Here are further thoughts.

> *Do not talk about a reference. You will dissipate it. The more you expose a reference to the light and watch other people's responses to it the less it will remain your own private, pristine thought. If you have a good reference — save it.*

A reference is best when specific. Don't just think something vaguely funny about the other person if you have to laugh at them. Imagine a penis is growing out of his forehead. This is crass but effective. Every time you look up at his forehead, there it is.

To feel sad, rather than thinking of yourself in a sad situation (emotion memory), it might work for you to think of someone else that you have deeply pitied, particularly a child. One single image can just melt you when the sufferer is innocent, helpless and hopeful.

When playing the action 'to humiliate' someone you might actually think of a bucket of manure being tipped all over them. You will gain that little extra focus and energy if as you speak to them you imagine that your action is having that effect on them. If you have a strong aversion to things anal, you might prefer to think of a bucket of water, or of a plate of spaghetti bolognaise dropped into their lap.

When playing an attacking kind of action (verbally), you might think of your words actually physically pushing them backwards. The thought only needs to be swift and confident to have an effect. Don't belabour it. Conversely with a comforting action you might imagine that your words are enveloping and soothing the other person.

INTELLECTUALISATION

The most common difficulty when learning to use references is that we tend to 'intellectualise'. This means that we tell ourselves we are tapping into a reference without actually doing so. We get stuck with just thinking of its name, for example, without actually experiencing the thought. You furrow your eyebrows and mutter to yourself 'I am thinking of the Eiffel Tower, I am thinking of the Eiffel Tower' but you don't see a thing. If you don't see it you can't respond to it. It is not an organic process, merely an intellectual one.

I found this a very difficult stage to go through. It just takes perseverance and practice. Using references to generate emotions instantly and efficiently is surely at the heart of all good acting. The solution, I think, has to do with not lingering on the thought for too long. All you need to refer properly is a fleeting moment, a flash. Once you start trying to hold the thought it will evaporate, it becomes intellectualised, and it will die. A long reference tends to be a series of short images, or notions revisited.

A PRACTICAL EXAMPLE

To give you an idea of very specific imagery, for what it is worth, I will give this personal example. I write this assuming that I won't be playing this role again. I was in a production of *Three Hotels* by Jon Robin Baitz, at the Ensemble Theatre in Sydney. My character, who was involved in pushing baby formula to African women, had lost a 16-year-old son some five years previously. My character's denial was so total that he had never discussed the tragedy with his wife nor had they ever mentioned the son's name since his death. At the end of the play I am alone in a hotel room, in the depths of despair, talking into a tape recorder. I utter my son's name, the first time inadvertently, then an instant later, in absolute agony.

What I thought of, immediately after the first mention of the forbidden name, was that a fish hook had suddenly caught in my heart and was being pulled out of my chest. As though this sudden, sharp and total pain at having uttered his name was ripping my heart out. Fighting against the pull of the hook was, in a sense, like trying to drag the notion of the dead child back inside me, back into the oblivion of the subconscious. I am using many words here to describe the simple idea, of a pain being dragged out of you which you desperately want to pull back inside of you. The notion of the sudden fish hook was enough to stop my breath and to trigger the second utterance of his name, which was more of a gasp of anguish, a howl, leading to the ensuing breakdown.

A moment later, in the last moments of the play, I was looking out of the window, at the celebrations of the Day of the Dead in this Mexican town. I was singing a lullaby and weeping. It was ambiguous whether the lullaby was to comfort my dead son or me. What was needed was for the audience to see the man, on a cloud of pain, gently trying to comfort an imaginary child, a wasted life. With the previous loading of pain still intact all I thought of as I sang the lullaby was of a baby in a cot, of tickling it gently under the chin, of tweaking a fat little toe, and finally tucking it in with a soft blue blanket while letting the song soothe it to sleep. I have no idea why all that enabled me to cry through the lullaby but it did. Notice not a single, genuine personal reference, only specific images. I know that five years ago this would not have worked. I would have needed the more personal stuff then.

Again, these references were gentle, quick flashes. You don't try to hold on to any one for any length of time. If you do it will evaporate, it will become intellectualised.

TO DO AND TO FEEL

It may have become apparent that references really have two distinct functions:

1. To make you feel
2. To make you do

The motivational techniques vaguely separate out into those that are better for generating feelings within you, like touching of images and memories; and those that enable you to play actions on other people, like usury and 'as if'.

Here is a rough rule which tends to hold for me:

A reference that makes you feel comes from inside your head (or heart).
A reference that makes you do comes from the other person's eyes.

(When talking directly to the audience you won't see their eyes. You will have to *listen* to what they are thinking.)

After a lot of practice while acting you will have these two concurrent activities humming away:

1. Dipping into your gladbag of images and memories to trigger your emotions as you need them, and

2. Continuously using the other actor, her delivery, her attitudes, her instantaneous responses, for usury — to justify the actions that you have to play on her.

The whole of acting then becomes a shadow game between what you say and do, and what you think. This hive of internal activity is simply to produce life-like responses in you.

WHEN THE IMAGINARY WORLD BECOMES REAL

In life a real event will occur, which will trigger thoughts and feelings in you, which will finally prompt your response. When acting it is a thought inside you that will generate your response. This, I think, is finally the essence of acting. It is responding to a lie, to something fake, to a thought that you yourself have chosen. But be very clear that only the stimulus need be fake. If you are clever, and pick the right thought, your response to it can be uncannily real. And herein lies the magic. If you can create plausible responses to the imaginary world around you then to the audience that imaginary world will become real.

Here is my drama teacher's favourite definition of the craft:

Acting is responding to an imaginary stimulus.

Having said all the foregoing, let me now confuse everything by adding: allow for some messiness. Allow imprecision as the thought forms. Don't try to lock it in — it will evaporate. Chekhov said of a Russian writer 'that he lacked those doubts that give talent grey hair'. Keep your references rich and full but don't try to over-define the edges.

In these pages I am trying to convey the sorts of events that actually occur inside the actor. But while performing it does not help to discuss things too much, to analyse, verbalise too much, even to yourself, because a lot of what you do is a sort of sleight of hand with your own brain, on the spur of the moment. The whole idea is to surprise yourself and to allow yourself to fly.

7
OBJECTS OF ACTIONS AND ADJUSTMENTS

Consider this scene. A child is wielding a broom around a garden path, learning to sweep. Her father is beside her actually sweeping away the leaves. They are both moving brooms around. What is the difference in their behaviour? It is so obvious, but how do you describe it?

Here is one way. The object of the child's action is the broom itself, learning to wield it. The object of the father's action is the path, to get it clean.

The thing to which you give most of your attention is the object of your action.

The father is preoccupied with the leaves on the garden path. They are the *object* of his action. He wants to get rid of them. He hardly notices how he is handling the broom. To him that is incidental; so it is an adjustment. To the child, that is the whole point of the exercise, to wrestle with the unruly handle, to learn to dominate it. So the object of the child's action is the broom. The leaves hardly come into it.

We have returned to the enormously important distinction between an action and an adjustment, referred to on page 29. As you can see, a powerful indicator to help us determine what an action is and whether an activity is an action or an adjustment, is to first of all find out what the object of your action is. Where is your attention? You can imagine how useful this is when trying to troubleshoot a moment that has gone wrong in a production. Are you concerned with the leaves or the broom handle? With the other person on stage with you or with the sound of your own voice?

There are many actors who adore to show the audience that they are acting, who like to play with the style and the voice, not as real characters but as 'part of the theatrical creation'. I'm afraid this is not my religion. For me a good performance seems effortless. The adjustments seem incidental. That is not to say that I don't like large, inventive characters. I just don't like to be reminded by the player that he or she is doing it. I am of the school that believes that in order to create magic you mustn't show the audience the trick. They will never believe Superman can fly if they can see the wires holding him.

Unlike British justice, acting should only ever be done. It should never be seen to be done.

I can hear you say, 'But hang on, what about astonishing performances that I have seen in the theatre which were enormously theatrical, self-conscious and absolutely riveting?'

COMMENTING ON THE ILLUSION

Stephen Berkoff is a wonderful case in point. His theatrical monologues are vibrant, challenging, brutal views of a tough society and of a lonely life. As an actor he has no difficulty in playing plausible characters, as can be seen from his cinema performances. However, he likes to challenge theatrical conventions. He toys with the fundamental elements of theatre and perception. I saw a performance of his one-man show called *One Man*. The last thing that he wanted to do here was to give his audience simple believable characters. On the contrary, he would create a moment and then immediately destroy it by commenting on it. He would draw attention to a whine in his voice, or to a particular move of the leg. He would repeat a particular attitude or mannerism, over and over, turning an incidental moment into a theatrical event. You eventually asked yourself, 'How can he keep us interested when he keeps shattering the illusion of what he is doing?' The question then becomes, what *is* he doing?

The answer is: he is entertaining *us*. *We* are the object of his action. He can afford to destroy the illusions of his story because his intention is not to sweep us into that imaginary world; it is to sweep us into the magic of this theatre, under his spell. This aspect of his performance is imperceptible. He does not make comment of his relationship with us nor of the fact that he is trying to mesmerise us. In this he allows us to see no strings.

Commenting reminds the audience that they are watching something premeditated. Consequently it does not belong to theatre which tries to believably create an imaginary world. But when the world it tries to create is the theatre itself, then sharing the artifice with the audience can be both effective and memorable.

> ## *PERICLES*
> There are occasions in more traditional theatre when the best option is to draw attention to the illusion, to admit we are acting. There are comedy scenes in Shakespeare, for example, whose puns and wit draw a very long bow today. They can produce in the audience that uneasy silence, filled with the difficult notion that perhaps they are meant to be laughing. But when the Bard decides to put in some laughs at a particular point in the play, a modern director is wise to take note. In a production of *Pericles*, directed by Toby Robertson in England in the seventies, I played, amongst other things, one of the three fishermen; it is a comedy scene. The director had set the whole play in a transvestite brothel in Mytelene (it was a brilliant production) and we fishermen played the scene as though it were our cabaret act, as clowns with red noses. We drew on the Marx Brothers, the Three Stooges, Chaplin, anything; falling, tumbling and frolicking our way through the scene. We did not alter the words; we just gave the audience more recognisable elements to laugh at. At heart we were saying to them, 'Yes, we are actors. This play is indeed by Shakespeare. This scene was hilarious 400 years ago. We are in the twentieth century. Shakespeare wanted laughs at this point in the show. We'll see what we can do for you here tonight.'

WORKING-IN THE ADJUSTMENTS

I have said elsewhere that the working-in of the adjustments is what takes the greatest amount of effort when preparing for a role, if the newly acquired accent or mannerisms are to look effortless, natural.

While you are learning a new adjustment, for a while it becomes an action.

At first you *play the action* to speak with an Italian accent, or to put on a limp.

We are creating magic. It is trickery. In performance we do pay attention to our adjustments. We have to be in control of how we deliver a line or throw a look; of the precise position of the body as it goes into a fall. That is what acting is. But our skills must be such that our attention to all these never becomes apparent.

CHILDREN ARE NOT AS GOOD ACTORS AS WE THINK

There is a group of people who have not yet learnt to handle their real life adjustments well. These are children under the age of, say, 10. We have spoken of the child wrestling with the broom.

There is a myth that children have an uncanny, innate skill for acting. This no doubt comes from the fact that without any training children can often give very credible performances. The normal explanations run along lines like: 'Children are less inhibited than adults, they are more imaginative, they are better mimics and that is why they can instantly act well.' These are all true but they ignore a crucial point.

The performance of an inexperienced actor and the behaviour of a five-year-old child have this in common: They both have to pay attention to their speech and gestures. Neither of them is good at handling adjustments yet. A child's whole life is taken up with learning behaviour, as it tries to wrap its tongue around simple phrases, as it puts on a frown or imitates a gesture. These acts are self-conscious. The child observes them as it performs them. Let me now draw your attention to the television where business men and women have decided to appear in their own ads. They also are often awkward in their line delivery, they also feel self-conscious about this arm gesture or this turn of the head, because they are not used to having to repeat a piece of behaviour over and over. They also are watching it as they do it.

The novice actor, insofar that he has to pay attention to his adjustments, behaves like a child. Consequently if the novice actor is an adult he may quite likely look a little mentally challenged — have a look at the ads! If the novice actor, however, is a child then its performance may very well look remarkably close to a real child's. Not only because children have that natural freedom. But because a child's awkwardness in real life looks similar to the awkwardness of inexperienced acting. Neither handles adjustments nimbly.

WHY DO MANY ACTORS HAVE FAKE COVERS?

There is a wide variety isn't there? Ranging from the brooding, mumbling Method-school cover to the flamboyant, over-articulated Classical persona.

All of us, of course, are a result of our genetic make-up, our upbringing, hobbies, our social, cultural, sporting and educational journey so far, and every inspiring influence of our lives.

In the course of becoming an actor, there is a point when you have to look at your own behaviour very closely. It is unavoidable.

OBJECTS OF ACTIONS AND ADJUSTMENTS

You become self-conscious — literally: conscious of self. As you watch your behaviour you are forced to revisit questions left behind in childhood and in your teens. What sort of person do I want to be? How do I want to appear? How do I want to behave? Now, at drama school, the questions are asked again, but with more insistence. Rare amongst professions, this one now gives you the opportunity to rethink your persona, to redesign your cover.

The result is often bizarre. Many actors end up looking fake, premeditated, as though they were always posing. One reason of course is that some people attracted to theatre have difficulties with their every day personae to begin with. That's why they want to act. They hope that new characters will camouflage their shyness or social shortcomings. But I have a feeling that the process of the acting class adds to the problem.

During acting exercises, as we try to reproduce life and miss slightly, we unconsciously look for approximations. We try to find simpler ways of representing behaviour. By cutting corners we end up with something a little fake. It is codified behaviour, stylised. But if the fakeness is in accordance with the general bias of the school, that is, if it leans towards the theatrical in a classical school, or is stern and meaningful in a naturalistic school, then it may very well be accepted by the rest of the class and the teacher as being 'close enough' to the real thing. We arrive at this stylisation out of self-protection, because it is daunting to constantly use the breathtaking subtleties of real life as a criterion for behaviour. And now a subtle shift occurs, an involuntary, subconscious decision is made. Rather than insist on bringing reality into acting, we choose to bring acting into real life. It is easier to reproduce this behaviour in class, and lo and behold, it even makes our interactions in *real life* easier. Glibber, slightly affected, but easier.

If you are a drama student I suggest that *the acting exercises were not meant to be a guide for your real life behaviour. They were meant to help you learn to reproduce it.*

You will never again be unselfconscious. But I suggest that you try to return to as natural a state of behaviour as possible, because the limits of your acting ability will be determined in part by how believable you can be in real life. No set of characteristics that you can invent for yourself can ever be as multifaceted, as rich or as spontaneous as what Mother Nature herself has given you.

There is nothing more powerful for the artist than a truthful base to start from.

> On the other hand there is a philosophy which says that it is better for would-be actors to increase their idiosyncrasies; to make themselves more distinctive, more original. Warren Mitchell once said to me that actors with big noses who want to have a nose job should make their noses bigger.

RESEARCH

Here is where the real enjoyment of working on a role begins. If your role exhibits characteristics or skills with which you are not familiar you will have to do research. It may be to learn an accent, or to become familiar with a sport or a musical instrument, or to observe a professional at work.

This is when you have an excuse to wangle your way into training with a famous football team, or to sit in the pit with the orchestra during an opera. This is when you get to peep into lives and backgrounds that you would otherwise never come in contact with. It is heaven.

SEE A PROFESSIONAL

If you are to play a doctor who has to give someone a routine medical examination — blood pressure, listening to the heart and lungs through the stethoscope — a couple of sessions with your friendly G.P. will make the difference between an audience naturally accepting the scene, and one which sits cringing in embarrassment for this poor actor who clearly doesn't know what she is doing.

When you go to observe a professional at work, a dentist, a doctor, a lawyer, the most striking things that hit you are what they take for granted and what they concentrate on. What is adjustment, and what is action. The way the dentist turns from his workbench to pick up the drill, the ease with which the doctor wraps the blood pressure strap around the patient's arm, are adjustments. These are the things that the actor will have to rigorously practice. It is so often what you don't seem to pay any attention to that makes the performance believable.

The professional's overall attitude, her bedside manner if you like, speaks volumes about the routine of her life. Why she does what she does and what she thinks about it. Watching her perform pieces of behaviour which are to us essentially alien, is what will give us a blanket of authority. We will *know* that this behaviour is legitimate because we actually saw someone behave like this.

ACCENTS

I won't go into how you learn special skills, such as handling a musical instrument or a football. Once you have found a skilled professional to help you, it is basically common sense. Nor will I discuss learning to mime a song well, or finding the right walk and then drilling it in. They just take a lot of hard work. But because of the number of times that I have had to learn to do foreign accents, for what it is worth, I will give you an idea of how I go about it.

Avoid using a stock accent that you acquired for a previous production. Unless your parents spoke like that, or you have managed to keep listening carefully to people who do, it is likely that your accent will have stultified and become a cliché. Nor is it wise to ask another actor how she would do it, unless she has that background herself. There is no better way to learn an accent than to find someone who comes from the place in question. If you don't know anyone personally ring the appropriate embassy or look in the phone book for clubs or centres where people from this background socialise. You may have to tape the voices of several different people from the same ethnic background before you find an accent that you and your director feel sounds appropriate.

Taping Them
Getting someone to talk into a tape recorder is not as difficult as it sounds. You will be surprised at people's willingness to co-operate with *art*.

When you switch on the tape recorder *do not* ask them to say something. They will freeze up. An easy trigger for conversation is to ask them about their childhood and up-bringing, and their arrival in this country. You may want them to pronounce words in their own language that you will need to say in the play. But *do not* ask them to read any of your English lines, because you are likely to end up with an amateur trying hard to read to you in their second language. This has nothing to do with the way they express themselves normally. Having recorded them, go home and listen to the tape. As the conversation progresses and as they warm to their subject you will hear how their heart speaks. That's what you want.

Listen First
Listen to specific differences in the vowel sounds and the consonants. Above all listen to the rhythms, the cadences, the unusual stresses. After becoming very familiar with the tape, approach your script.

Approaching the Script
Look at a line and try to imagine how your subject would say it. You will be chasing all through the tape to hear how he pronounced 'a' as in hat. For the first few days it may be back-breaking research, sound by sound, moment by moment. After a few days, however, our associative memory begins to help. It provides a generalised sense of what sounds right and what doesn't. Don't trust it completely, keep going back to the tape, because your memory will try to trick you by cutting corners, by trying to make things easier for you. But as the days go on, your ear will become uncannily attuned to the prototype on the tape. Start to ad-lib. Do 'Mary Had A Little Lamb' in your new accent. Do 'The Lord's Prayer'. Play

OBJECTS OF ACTIONS AND ADJUSTMENTS

with it, work it in. Eventually you will find a key phrase or word which will somehow encapsulate for you this whole speech pattern. You will find that when you have been away from the script for a while just saying that key phrase will almost automatically click you back into the accent.

NOW learn the lines.

If you start to learn them before you have a good grasp of the accent you will have to re-learn sounds that you have already begun to memorise. Very messy.

LEARNING LINES

One of the most frequent questions asked of actors is 'How do you remember your lines?' I can't believe that I am actually going to tell you what I do. (Another frequent question of course used to be 'What work do you do during the day?')

You are very welcome to skip this section.

In real life we rarely think of the words that we use when we speak, rather we think of the thought being carried by them. The same should apply when acting. Speaking the lines is an adjustment.

You read the whole script, then you read it again and then again. You think about it, nurse it, establish a relationship with it, make friends with it, grow to love it. (If you hate it you shouldn't be doing it. *Find* things to love about it.) In the next chapter we will discuss script analysis, and see how that process alone is a huge step towards absorbing the text. Close inspection of the interactions and developments of the story breaks the hard ground. It moulds the phrases into thoughts, which will eventually make it easier to digest the words.

Here we go. Read the other person's line, and then your following line. You know the thought behind your line, you know what it means. Cover it up with a piece of paper and try to say it. Have a peek and try again. Relate it to the previous speech. Cover yours and try again. If your speech is long, break it up into sentences and say each sentence by heart, once or twice is enough. Having said it leave it now and go on to the other person's next speech. After going through the whole script once, having said each individual line by heart the seeds are planted. You are still far from knowing it, but you can now start to tackle the script a scene at a time, reading the other person's line and trying to answer with your own.

The same process applies to a one-person show except that there, there are no other people's speeches. During rehearsals for my favourite one-person play, *Sky*, written for me by John Misto, I used to come home and say to my wife 'I've only got two speeches in this show. Act 1 and Act 2.' The secret of long speeches is, like anything else, to break it down into manageable pieces. Learn each sentence by covering it up and trying to say it. Then do sweeps of that page, and then sweeps of the whole scene, and finally runs of the whole play.

If the role is large, make a timetable, otherwise you will end up spending too much time on one scene at the expense of another. It is also crucial to learn all parts of the script at approximately the same rate so that, as you learn the lines, you also develop an overall understanding of your character.

Lines are Thoughts
At the heart of learning lines is the fact that you are not learning a huge string of words at all, you are learning a thought sequence.

It takes a lot of words to convey a simple thought.

There we have 11 words. But see how simple the thought is? Once you've learnt the thought it is only a question of memorising the writer's exact wording.

But it's the thought that counts.

Another six words for one more thought. It should not take you long to memorise these 17 words because they have been introduced as two simple thoughts.

If you drive a car think of a long journey that you often make, say of over 100 kilometres. If you had to write down the whole set of visual cues that you use to guide you through that journey you would fill a book. 'Cross this first street, turn left at the park, go wide at the sharp corner in case of oncoming traffic, follow the park right around, turn right at Wayne's house and immediate left over that little hill, I hate that little hill, you can never see what's coming' … Yet when the cues come up you have no trouble in remembering the next bit of the journey. It took you a while to learn the whole sequence, but having learnt it, it is not difficult to repeat. It is exactly the same with a script.

ELUSIVE OBJECTS OF ACTIONS

We have touched on cases where it was not clear what the object of the action was, such as when listening to music, or when a tennis player berates himself. I will end this chapter toying with this tantalising topic.

Recall that each action is a little thought package that we send to the object of the action, usually another person. But we can also send these packages internally — from one part of the brain to another.

Timothy Gallwey in his book *The Inner Game* suggests that we have two parts when playing sports — Self 1, the coach, and Self 2, the player. When we buck ourselves up it is indeed as though there was one part of the brain (Self 1) sending good reasons to the other part of the brain (Self 2) to show why we shouldn't be scared. Here Self 2 is the object.

The same principle applies to internal events, like trying to remember a name or trying to decide between alternatives. In trying to remember the name the little searcher in the brain flicks through the memory bank. To me the memory bank is here the object of the action.

When trying to make a decision we have a little arbiter in the brain looking at the two alternatives, weighing up their consequences and their relative merits. I would call the alternatives the objects of this action. However we define these events, we can see that something internal is clearly trying to be achieved.

But there are pieces of behaviour which are not adjustments because they are too deliberate, nor do they seem to be actions in that they don't seem to try to affect anything: listening to music, grieving, looking at the stars, admiring a car, chatting to a friend.

A man is sitting with his head in his hands two days after the death of his father. He is crying. What is he doing? The act is not unconscious, it is not automatic. It would seem that he is deliberately sitting there suffering. Is this a case where a deliberate activity does *not* try to change anything?

No. He is dealing with memories, perhaps kissing them goodbye. He may be dealing with guilt — what he should have said, what he should have done; not to mention the unspeakable guilt of the little corner of his heart that didn't love his father. He is dealing with anger at the loss, at the change in his life. He is grappling with the pain. All these sensations are the objects of his actions and he is trying to ride them, to make sense of them and finally to regain equilibrium.

What do you change when you listen to Schubert or look at the stars in the night sky? You expose your mind to sounds and sights that may intellectually inform you, or that may emotionally soothe you. Let me be schmaltzy: I would say that what is really being touched here is your soul.

Finally, chatting to a friend about absolutely nothing would seem to be the most futile activity imaginable. But we have no more powerful way to affirm our own existence than by sharing a common view of the world with another person. Patrick White in *The Tree of Man* writes 'Then Amy Parker settled down to being with her friend, to drink the pot dry, to the dregs of intimacy. The neighbour made her, by turns, satisfied, anxious, contemptuous, forgiving, superior, ignorant, pure, hypocritical, giggly, bored, breathless, possessive, even cruel; yet all these phases were impersonations by her true self, that loved the lives they had shared on that road of ruts and raggedy trees.'

8

THE SCRIPT

This chapter will address the age old problem at rehearsals, 'I'm not sure how to say this line.'

There is a lovely old story attributed to a fine actor called Michael Bryant who was around the Royal Shakespeare Company in the seventies. One day during rehearsals, the distinguished director, Peter Brook, took Michael aside and they had a very long chat. It was about Michael Bryant's character, about the text, and about the iambic pentameter (the rhythm of Shakespeare's verse). After about 40 minutes Michael Bryant got up and said, 'Alright, Peter, now I understand about the "dum de-dum de-dum de-dum de-dum". But what's it mean?'

THE WRITTEN WORD

We have a strange relationship with words. On the one hand they mean everything, on the other they mean nothing. 'I'll kill that dog!' How often has that been said in gentle, respectable homes, by kind-hearted people? The dog, of course, usually dies many years later of natural causes.

We rarely say what we mean, and even more rarely say what we feel. Yet when we are reading, the words explode directly in our heads and convey images and meaning. Our literature and legal systems hinge totally on this fact. In court lawyers will pounce on the precise wording of what someone was heard to say three years ago. 'Yes, your Honour, I definitely heard him say, "I'll kill that dog".'

And yet the moment you write down what someone said its meaning becomes ambiguous, because *written words do not convey intent.* When we read a novel there is no problem. The silent words convey images. We have a general 'feel' for how the character in the story sounds. This feeling is of course very personal. What's more we are never pushed to actually describe what that sound is. We just know what the line means. As soon as you read a script out loud it is different. As soon as you have an organic voice to utter those words there is a new heart involved. The trick is now to make sure that this heart beats in harmony with the writer's.

In life we do not respond to words, so much as the thought behind them — the intent. Had we been there when the dog was scolded we would have known that it was in no danger. So while we depend on the author's words for the whole play it is the momentary thoughts behind the words that will trigger the audience.

Words are thought carriers but they are not the thought.

It is the actor's job to correctly reunite the thoughts that the writer meant with the words that he wrote.

Script Driven vs Situation Driven

The easiest way to approach a script is to acknowledge it is a script. The thinking is along the lines, 'We will have people here talking, saying the words that were written by Anton Chekhov or William Shakespeare or some other genius and by virtue of the fact that they are the words of this genius we expect you to sit up and listen. We will do what we can to make the experience relevant and interesting but at the end of the day, it *is* a script.'

I have a problem with this. To me it is defeatist. It is cheating.

It is unlikely that Chekhov or Shakespeare wrote their pieces in this spirit. I think that they simply tried to write rattling good tales of situations or relationships and let the events speak for themselves. We do them a greater courtesy by trying to present their scripts as though they simply evolve out of the action and the situation. Allow the audience to start from the premise that there is no script — only a situation. And that as a result of people's needs and their interactions things are necessarily said, and so a script just seems to evolve. It is certainly the way that Laurence Olivier and Franco Zeffirelli directed their films of *Hamlet*, in contrast to Tony Richardson's version.

Phrases like 'I don't know how I should say this line' and 'What can I do with this line to make it interesting?' sound as though there were infinite possibilities. There are not. Once we become familiar with the life of this character, once we realise what he or she is up to at this moment, how they operate and what has just happened, there will emerge very clear guidelines as to 'how to say this line'. It is not immediately obvious, but a large part of the answer to such simple questions lies not in the immediate moment being addressed, but in an overall concept of the play.

THE SPINE OF THE PLAY

To arrive at a concept we can start by asking some simple questions like: when was the piece written, under what circumstances? What was the writer exposing or getting off her chest? What was she actually trying to say? Does it have any relevance now? If so, what? If you wanted to put the whole play's statement into one phrase what would that phrase be?

Victor Hugo's classic novel *Les Misérables*, on which the musical was based, is undoubtedly a novel about the horrendous social injustices of eighteenth and nineteenth century France. But behind the background of the struggle towards a French republic and the heroism of a fair-minded man (Jean Valjean) and the relentless pursuit of him by another (Javert) and the unspeakable defencelessness of a single mother (Éponine) and the futile stand of the students at the barricades, and the love story, and the amoral evil of Thénardier; behind all these themes, for me there lingers one overriding message from Victor Hugo: that it is little people like you and me who create history. Vast changes, social upheaval, revolutions and ultimately progress are not brought about solely by the kings and the generals whose names appear in the history books but by the poor, the humble, the downtrodden — namely, in French 'les misérables'. Hugo continuously presents the ordinary flawed human being with such respect, with such dignity and compassion, that he leaves us with a lingering feeling that there exists in all of us a human spirit that can withstand all suffering, in order to eventually make the world a better place.

A tenet like, 'It is little people who change the world' is what we call *the spine of the play*.

The spine of *Hamlet* might be, 'The quest for revenge is ultimately self-destructive'.

It may seem indelicate to take a vast, intricate, multifaceted work of art and try to reduce it to one single statement. But the process is useful. When faced with a million dazzling elements this is a way of putting them into some kind of context; it is a way of giving us a starting point. I will go so far as to say that the precise spine we decide on is not as important as the fact that we have chosen one. Within limits, any spine is better than no spine. The members of the audience don't necessarily have to know what the spine is. They may only end up with a vague awareness of it; we are not trying to send them a 'message'. But for the director and cast, having decided on a spine will give the work a coherence.

Making the Script Work

I have spoken to people after seeing a play which has had a distinguished track record and won literary prizes, and I have heard them say, 'It's not a very good play, is it? But the acting was good.'

One can only conclude that: *It is easier to look like a good actor than to make the script work.*

It is fortunate for us actors that it is difficult for the untrained eye to identify whether the weakness lies in the script, the direction or the acting.

When people say that the acting was good they generally mean little more than that the actors seemed assured, committed and, on the moment, plausible. It has little to do with the psychological journey of the character, or an understanding of the relationship between distant events in the play. In this respect audiences are very generous — they often give the actors the benefit of the doubt.

By saying that the *play* wasn't good, people tend to mean that they couldn't relate to it, that they didn't care about anyone in it, that scenes seemed repetitious, implausible, illogical, and that in the crucial climactic scenes they were looking at their watches. If the play was in fact well constructed something has obviously gone wrong.

The problem is often that there was no clear view of the panorama. No concept of the story's shape and major crisis points. To move the audience, to let them experience what it was that the writer intended requires an understanding of what drives the drama — where the engine is. What causes what, where the climaxes are, where the surprises are, and how to lead up to them. We must generate a sense of never repeating an emotional moment. Each one should lead us into a slightly new state so that there is continual development.

In other words:

1. We need to have a clear understanding of the spine of the play,
2. How each scene contributes to that spine, and
3. How each moment fits into that scene.

Without this vision the best of plays can degenerate into a series of arbitrary, disconnected events. Scenes can become repetitious, the play mediocre and the evening long.

The Director's Choice

A ship can have only one captain and a play or film can have only one director. The vision, the interpretation is finally his or hers. It does not hurt to do one's own homework, to carry out one's own enquiry and preparation. But one must remain clear that in the final instance the thrust, the style, the meaning of the piece are decided by the director.

Your own work is never wasted. It gives you a clearer context from which to take in what the director is giving. And it is a joy to be shown a slant that one had not thought of, to have one's interpretation expanded, broadened, enriched by new associations. On the other hand Sir Ralph Richardson in a television interview, when asked, 'What do you think of directors?' answered, 'I don't talk to them very much', and disappeared out of shot.

There are often good reasons for a director to not simply produce what would seem to be the face value meaning of a play. There may be a theme in the play which was not central when the play was written but which has great relevance today and which the director may want to highlight.

In a brand new work the director often collaborates with the writer and advises where she feels the play *should* be heading, what should be expanded and omitted. In this instance the director has first hand input into the spine of the play.

Finally, the director may choose to distort the spine simply in the name of exploration; for the sheer joy of it; to find a new slant in a play which has been done to death. It is important that art should be always fresh, innovative and challenging. My only reservations are when the choices become incestuous — when the play is designed more to impress the industry, other directors and artists, than to communicate with the audience. When that happens we have lost sight of our reason for being on the stage.

THE LAST NOTE IS THE KEY

To discover what the spine of the play is is not unlike deciding what key a piece of music is in — you look at the final note. Because that is the key. The last moments, the final reverberation often indicates the intention of the whole play.

Hamlet

I will give a thumb-nail sketch of the play *Hamlet*. Forgive me if you know it well. Hamlet was the son of the king of Denmark. Before the play begins Hamlet's uncle, Claudius, murdered Hamlet's father (Claudius' brother), married Hamlet's mother and made himself king. By the end of the first act the Ghost of Hamlet's father has appeared to Hamlet, told him of Claudius's terrible deed and asked Hamlet to avenge him.

Hamlet becomes obsessed with the desire for revenge. On the

one hand he contemplates suicide. On the other he stages a play depicting a murder very similar to that of his father, and invites the whole court to the performance, including his uncle, Claudius. He wants to observe Claudius's reaction for signs of guilt. The guilt is confirmed. Throughout the play Hamlet dithers and vacillates and is finally responsible for the murder of an old man, Polonius, thinking it was his uncle. Polonius's daughter, Ophelia, who Hamlet once loved, goes mad and drowns herself. In the last moments of the play Hamlet's mother, as well as Claudius, Ophelia's brother Laertes, and Hamlet himself, in one way or another are all killed. The stage is strewn with bodies. In the final moments it is a visitor, Fortinbras, who comments on the spectacle of carnage on the stage as being more appropriate to a battlefield than to a home. The final glow is of wasted lives.

We have a story then of a tortuous quest for revenge, culminating in absolute catastrophe. I have no doubt Shakespeare's spine is along the lines that the quest for revenge is ultimately self destructive. 'If you seek revenge dig two graves' is an old Chinese proverb.

In Laurence Olivier's film there is no Fortinbras. The character has been cut. And the last moments focus on the glory of Hamlet, because of the wonderful king that he *might* have been had he lived. He is carried ever higher up the ramparts of the castle to be saluted and paid appropriate respect. At the beginning of the film, Olivier calls it 'a tragedy about a man who could not make up his mind'. And certainly the themes of plans gone wrong, indecision and unfortunate circumstance are there. But in the last moments the film is an unabashed glorification of the character Hamlet (and by association perhaps of the man playing him?). It is wonderful showbusiness, it is a riveting film, but it does seem slightly at variance with what was indicated by the script. At no point in the film (or play) is it suggested that Hamlet would have made a great king. Whereas Shakespeare has constructed an elaborate and convincing web of circumstances to suggest that the relentless quest for revenge will bring disaster.

But then another ten thousand directors would come up with another ten thousand concepts. And in all of them you will tend to find that the last note gives you the key.

THE SPINE OF YOUR CHARACTER

After the spine of the play another useful concept is to identify the overall aim of your character through the course of the play. What

THE SCRIPT

does he or she want, what drives them? What do they think would make them happy?

Hamlet's spine might be: to correct the world.

MAKE FRIENDS WITH YOUR CHARACTER

You cannot begin until you can justify what your character does in the play — their moral stand. How difficult this is for you depends on your own background and beliefs, and what your character has to do in the play. If there are difficulties, read the play over a couple of times and think about your character's up-bringing, perceptions, defences. Gradually you should come to an understanding, then an acceptance and finally a justification for what he or she does. Learn to breathe in their world view. Only then can you really start working on the play.

THE SCENIC SPINE

The writer will have taken twists and turns to tell the story, but there will be an overall structure to the play. This scene is needed at this point in order to set up that aspect of the plot so that when a particular event happens it will be plausible that this character will do such and such.

Every scene starts at one point and finishes at another. The sum total of all such scenic journeys of course gives us the play. It is important to be very clear about what precisely the journey of each scene is. What is it that the audience needs to have seen happen for this part of the story to be told? How does this scene contribute to the overall story, why is it essential?

(If you can't find a good reason for it being there then you have a problem. It is like finding a lever in your car engine that does not seem to be doing anything. Car manufacturers do not generally put gratuitous levers under the bonnet.)

Act I scene 5 of *Hamlet* is the scene when the Ghost of Hamlet's father tells Hamlet everything — how he was murdered etc. A possible spine for this scene would be: to point Hamlet in the right direction.

THE CHARACTER'S SPINE IN A SCENE

Knowing what the scene is meant to do gives a clue to what your own character's function in that scene is.

It is a great help to determine what your character wants to achieve in each scene. You get this from considering where your character has come from at the beginning of the scene, what his expectations are, what he achieves by the end of the scene. The way your character negotiates his way through the scene tells you a lot about what he was trying to achieve.

It often happens that a character's spine changes half-way through a scene. In Act I scene 5, Hamlet's spine when listening to the Ghost is to grapple with what he is hearing, to deal with this new and horrible information. But when the Ghost has gone, it is now to get a pledge of silence from his friends, Horatio and Marcellus, who also saw the Ghost. He wants absolute secrecy from them.

When a scene naturally breaks up like this, and it can be very much more subtle than in this example, be aware of it and simply be clear on what your character's aims are in the different segments.

PLOTTING ACTIONS

Having mapped out what the scenes in the play are doing and how they each contribute to the overall spine we now come to the individual speeches and moments within each scene. We are now at grassroots level. These are the moments the play is made up of. These are the elements of timing. To determine what is happening at each moment we go through a procedure called Plotting Actions.

This consists of looking at each speech and going beyond what the character feels at that point, and going beyond what the speech means. We now try to decide what the character *does*. We try to work out what action he or she is playing. What effect do they want to see in the other person as a result of saying this line? You try to give this little action a name, a phrase. It is always verbal, a doing phrase, along the lines suggested in the Appendix. Each such action is called 'a beat action'. Deciding what name to call each action is what we call 'plotting the actions'.

You can see that we are already bracing ourselves against the trap of showing our feelings, by deliberately thinking in terms of what it is that the character is *doing* to the world around. The process is gruelling, painstaking and yet exhilarating. In defining the character's preoccupation, what he is trying to achieve at any moment, we are forced to consider not only this scene but the whole play and the deepest recesses of the character's psyche.

As with anything, practice makes life very much easier. And after a few years you will develop a shorthand, you will not need to name every action. You will quickly 'know' what your character is doing and be able to play it honestly. To get to this stage takes time. What will remain indelible is the ability to instantly give a name to a piece of behaviour when required. This becomes very useful when repairing a moment that has ceased to work, or when you want to analyse a particularly interesting piece of interaction between people.

This section would not be complete if we didn't have a quick example of plotting actions. I will use a scene from David Mamet's play *Sexual Perversity in Chicago* (page 22 in my 1974 Methuen edition). I use Mamet because apart from being entertaining I feel that he has probably the best ear in the English language for how we actually communicate. I would ask you to read his dialogue first and only then come back and read the actions that I have suggested (printed on the right). Remember that the names of the actions are not tossed off lightly. They are weighed up, chewed over and subsequently questioned at each stage of rehearsal. And they are personal.

All we need to know is that Danny and Deborah are in their twenties. Otherwise the scene is self explanatory.

The Library. DEBORAH *is seated, working.* DANNY *cruises her and so on.*
DANNY: Hi. .... to get her attention
DEBORAH: Hello. .... to keep him at bay
DANNY: I saw you at the Art Institute. .... to break the ice (casually)
DEBORAH: Uh huh. .... to let him dangle
DANNY: I remembered your hair. .... to ally
DEBORAH: Hair memory. .... to chop him off at the knees
DANNY: You were in the Impressionists room. .... to pinpoint
   [*Pause.*]
   Monet... .... to impress her
   [*Pause.*]
DEBORAH: Uh huh. .... to let him freeze
DANNY: You're very attractive. I like the way you look. .... to level with her
   [*Pause.*]
DANNY: You were drawing in charcoal. .... to go back to the art side of her
   It was nice.
   [*Pause.*]
   Are you a student at the Art Institute? .... to try to get a toe in the door
DEBORAH: No, I work. .... to discourage
DANNY: Work, huh? ... work. .... to deal with this blind alley
   [*Pause.*]
DANNY: I'll bet you're good at it. .... to cling onto the initiative
   [*Pause.*]
   Is someone taking up a lot of your time these days? .... to feel her out
DEBORAH: You mean a man? .... to call a spade a spade
DANNY: Yes, a man. .... to stand his ground
DEBORAH: I'm a Lesbian. .... to clarify
DANNY: [*Pause.*] .... to reassemble the troops
   As a physical preference, or from .... to convert this to a
   political beliefs?   philosophical discussion

There are a couple of things worth mentioning here.

1. On Danny's second line I have included a colour, 'casually', after the action. This is common practice, but I generally try to find actions which inherently contain the right colour so that you don't have to name it. That feels more efficient — it is easier to play.

2. It is Deborah's subsequent dialogue which tells us that her first 'Hello' is a discouraging, or at best non-committal, action. The line itself tells us little. What follows will often clarify what is happening at a particular moment.

3. All pauses contain actions but they are not often plotted. I have plotted one here because in this particular pause there is a lot happening. It is what I call a 'Corner' in the scene — a sharp change in direction for the character (see Chapter 9). After Deborah tells him that she is a Lesbian he pauses. During that pause I suggest that he is reassembling his troops. By that I mean that he has been completely disoriented by her mischievousness

and he has to totally reassess the situation before he can continue.

4. The names of actions can take many forms. They are only limited by your own imagination and vocabulary. On occasion they can be longer than the line they are describing. Nothing matters as long as they evoke an appropriate idea of what the character is doing at that moment.

TIPS ON PLOTTING

1. Plot actions which will help keep your attention off yourself. For example Deborah's second 'Uh huh' in the above scene could well be called 'to show disinterest'. But where would she have to look to see whether she was showing disinterest? At herself, to see what she was showing. Far safer to call it 'to let him freeze', an action on him.

2. Plot actions that stimulate, which fire the imagination rather than those which are boringly precise. 'To take the wind out of his sails' is better than 'to dissuade'.

3. Plot actions that lead you forward, that urge you to follow through. Avoid those that, once played, die on you. If 'to defy' is appropriate use that in preference to 'to warn'. Once you've given the warning there is nothing else you can do. Whereas 'to defy' implies a more on-going activity. Interestingly enough actions which tend to make you look at yourself, like 'to show disinterest' and 'to put on a brave face', also tend to stop dead once played.

4. As discussed (page 42) do not plot the action 'to be'.

5. Do not plot the actions 'to ask', 'to tell' or 'to explain'. *Plot actions which are specific rather than general.* These three are so general that they are meaningless. They tell you nothing about the specific transaction occurring. Every action in the Mamet scene falls into one of these three categories. When Danny says, 'Are you a student at the Art Institute?' calling that action 'to try to get a toe in the door' tells us so much more than if we'd called it 'to ask'.

In general instead of 'to ask' see if you can call it 'to check', 'to test', 'to feel out', 'to seek clarification'.

Instead of 'to tell' see if you can use things like 'to paint the picture', 'to fill the other person in', 'to clarify', 'to confide'.

There is no more boring conversation than when giving information to the man at the Motor Registry Office. But even then you don't play the action 'to tell'. You play actions like 'to begrudge the information', 'to spell it out', 'to repeat', 'to bear with this idiot', 'to correct', 'to send him up'.

6. Plot actions that will make you do what the audience needs to see. Often the action that the audience needs to see is not the best

thing for you to think of doing. You would never need to plot this in a script, but if the audience needed to see you puffing, the action you should think of is 'to try to catch your breath' not 'to puff'. If you try to catch your breath you will puff, whereas if you think of puffing you will just feel silly.

One day, in class, while Hayes was directing a scene he suggested to a student that 'to reassure' might be appropriate for a particular line. I was sure that the character should in fact have been playing something more like 'to undermine'. When I asked Hayes about it afterwards he said that because the actress in real life was so unreassuring, when she plays 'to reassure' it will look like 'to undermine'. If he had asked her to play 'to undermine' it would have looked like 'to castrate'.

7. A long speech is a series of short actions. We may choose to give each one a name or lump the whole thing together. It's up to you. Giving the whole thing a single name allows for a looser, freer approach.

A useful thought to bear in mind with a long speech is that if the character had achieved what they wanted after the first beat of the speech they would not have gone on. It implies that every moment in a long speech is trying to complete what has been left undone by the previous section. It is a useful notion for keeping the life going through an intricate monologue.

At first sight, one can be forgiven for thinking that plotting actions is merely an elaborate way of reminding us how to say the line. Nothing could be further from the truth. When you play an action you try to affect the other person. When you give a line reading you are doing something to yourself.

PLOTTING ACTIONS HELPS YOU MEMORISE

Quite apart from the great functional values of plotting actions the process is a great help in memorising the dialogue. Instead of thinking in terms of long strings of words we end up memorising coherent thought sequences. Once the sequence of mental and emotional processes has become familiar it is simply a question of memorising the precise wording used by the writer, which is by now so much easier.

ACTIONS WILL CHANGE

You will find that as you become more familiar with the script your concept of the actions changes. When starting off and pondering over what your character is doing to the other person at this moment you will come up with one answer. But a couple of weeks down the track when you can say the lines much more fluently you will find that in slow motion you plotted yourself into mental nooks and crannies that your character would never go into at speed. I confess to a certain clumsiness in not being able to avoid going over the script and constantly altering the actions as the picture becomes more clear. To date I have found no alternative but to start slowly. Here is an example from the television sit-com *Mother and Son*.

In this episode my character, Robert, the despicable dentist, has a new prospective mistress called Carmen. He tells his wife, Liz, that he is going out to take his senile old mother, Maggie, for a drive. He drives Maggie to Carmen's flat, leaves her sitting in the car outside while he goes in to chat up Carmen. She now tells him that she will only go to bed with him if he is open about their relationship, and if he tells his wife, and if Carmen can meet her.

ROBERT: OK, I'll tell Liz and I'll tell her tonight. But ... what if she doesn't mind about you and me, but she doesn't want to meet you?
CARMEN: I want to meet her.
ROBERT: What if she wrote you a letter and said she didn't mind.

I first called this last line 'to test'. My final name for it was 'to try to strike a compromise'. 'To test' establishes the general area that Robert is playing in at that moment. But it is generalised, bald and obvious. 'To try to strike a compromise' on the other hand, presumes a position of strength that he simply does not have. Carmen is a strong woman, he wants to go to bed with her, and his ploy is totally transparent. With this action he again shows us his hollow, hopeless confidence. The action felt funny and I think it is pretty well what I ended up playing.

Plotting actions in isolation is a first step of familiarisation with the script. Once rehearsals start these actions will change again. What you call the action, the way you think of it, depends not only on what you want to achieve but also on the state of the other person.

If your action is to stop the car you will do one set of things if you are travelling at 20 kilometres per hour and quite another if you're doing 120 kilometres per hour.

The actions you plot will depend on what the other actors are doing and on the taste of the director. Nothing is fixed until rehearsals are over and the audience is watching. And as we shall see, at that point a whole new world will open up.

ART NEEDS LOGIC

All this analysis of scripts and plotting of actions may seem cold and calculated. You may feel that it lacks spontaneity and inspiration. This overlooks the fact that the very naming of actions requires human insight. Understanding the script needs sympathy and identification with the writer's vision. But it is only the beginning. It is at rehearsals that the piece begins to come to life — inspiration comes from interaction with the other actors and with a sense of flow and speed. Finally, the ultimate insights will come when we interact with the audience once the play opens. But for inspiration and insights to be most beneficial we need first to have done our homework.

Just as you cannot be a good scientist without using intuition so you cannot be a good artist without using logic.

An actor needs to have an understanding of human nature, of script structure and audience dynamics. But for an artist, logic need not be analytical. The artist needs simply to acknowledge and respect organic truth, have a sense of living things and have an appreciation of the audience's world view.

The whole point of plotting actions is to help us
- observe,
- identify, and
- reproduce

the interactions that happen in real life.

On a radio programme called *Books and Writing* on the ABC I heard the following parable. A little girl asks her grandmother,

Q: What is the difference between a lie and a story?

A: A lie tries to cover up the truth. A story tries to expose it.

9
REHEARSALS

This is where we make the giant leap from conception to realisation. Up till now we have been pondering about the play. We have been testing it, walking around it, prodding it and sizing it up. We have been learning the lines, preparing special skills, inspecting the background and laying foundations. Now we come to do it.

(I love the Robert Mitchum quote, 'Acting's easy. They tell you where to stand, what to say, where to look. You don't have to do anything.' Behind that laid-back exterior of course was a meticulous professional, who has given some excellent performances.)

The prospect, now, of actually doing it is always daunting. In the first days of rehearsals it is inconceivable that in four weeks' time we will actually be performing this play, in front of an audience, *without a script.*

The fear is well-founded. It is hard to play a role well. If, by the time you open, you cannot take the audience through all the appropriate moments at the pace that *they* need, you will lose them, they will be bored, and your performance will fall in a heap. That, in a nutshell, is the problem. Close behind is the industry's catch-cry 'You are only as good as your last performance.'

At the start of rehearsals everything is very exciting. For one thing, you're in work! The cast gathers, the director gives his or her introductory remarks, the designer unveils the model of the set and displays drawings of the costumes. Then we have the first reading of the play. It tends to be a self-conscious, fumbling and yet bonding affair. It pretends to be casual but in fact carries enormous weight. It is the first overall indication the director has of the chemistry he has put together with this cast.

As days go by each actor brings in the homework they have done; accents, walks — whatever, and we work on the scenes. Everyone is brave and will try anything. Every silly idea is allowed. Moments are discovered, pieces of behaviour are wrestled with, scenes are explored, directed, redirected, moves evolve and become set. Decisions are made about props and costumes. In order to get used to them we have temporary coats, skirts, plates to play with until the real stuff arrives. Obvious comedy moments are inspected, fleshed out, justified and brought to life, while totally unexpected bits of business also explode onto the scene. While most of these will light up the place for a moment and then disappear without trace, some will survive and become part of the show. Serious emotional moments also begin to quiver and take life, and scenes take shape and start to flow. It is an awkward, glaring, exposing, bonding experience. The actors impress one another yet again with all their different skills.

When things are going well it is hard not to have a sense of excitement mingled in with the danger. There is always that silent, incorrigible possibility that this might in fact turn out to be a very good show.

And then, something happens. Things begin to slightly distort. An indefinable shadow falls over bits of the performance. The effect is brittle, dry, grotesque.

CRYSTALLISATION

Some of funniest bits of business are no longer funny. Not because we have become used to them but because *they* have changed. A funny look that someone had two weeks ago is now a grimace. Something which was once said with delicious venom has now become a clever vocal inflection. A trip now looks premeditated, a fumble deliberate. A sad moment has become sentimental. People are pushing their feelings, and others are answering each other before they could possibly have heard what the other was saying. Moments of surprise are glossed over.

What is happening?

Until now everyone had been listening to one another because nobody knew what was coming next. Nothing was premeditated because nobody was quite sure of what they were going to do themselves. Everything was fresh. Now, it often happens after two or three weeks of rehearsals, amongst the rich, developing performances are these little traces of atrophy, of crystallisation.

Even at this early stage of the proceedings we come face to face with a fundamental rule of life:

Acting consists of two distinct skills:
1. creating the role, and
2. maintaining it.

Ironically the problem we have struck is that rehearsals are working. We *are* becoming familiar with the show. At each moment we know what we have to say, what we are meant to feel, what we are about to do, and worst of all, what the other person is about to do. You would think that this new confidence, this new information, would help. Far from it. We now face the most fundamental problem in all of acting:

How do you play the present moment as though you didn't know what was coming, when you do?

I think all those examples of shortcuts mentioned above, this crystallisation of behaviour, manifests itself in no more than three principal ways. They are all versions of the great enemy of acting: *anticipation*.

Playing the Form

Because we have now decided how to play the various moments there is a powerful tendency to do just that. It is an urge to directly manufacture the external trappings of the behaviour without going through the internal processes which gave rise to them. We call this 'playing the form'. A stance, a gesture, a facial expression, a line reading, are manufactured directly, by-passing the sequence of thoughts which originally generated them. The skill of people like Peter Sellers, Jacques Tati and Michael Richards (Kramer in *Seinfeld*), was in being able to produce extraordinary pieces of physical behaviour while maintaining a clear connectedness with the events that are supposed to have triggered them.

The problem with playing the form is that no matter how skilled you are you can never reproduce all the tiny little events that happen to your being when it genuinely lives. A clever line reading alone, without the accompanying thoughts and emotions, without the inner life, remains a line reading.

Dame Edith Evans was once asked by a young actor, 'Dame Edith, why don't we get that laugh any more, when I hand you that cup of tea?' She answered, 'Because, dear boy, you're not handing me a cup of tea. You're handing me a laugh.'

The solution is to re-focus onto the *actions* that we were playing which gave rise to the behaviour, and to revisit those thoughts that generated those attitudes.

Playing the Colours

Here, we are intent on reproducing the feelings directly, to *show* them. This is B-Grade movie acting again, as mentioned earlier. You know the sort of thing. The hero has been fatally shot (not before time) and his lady is weeping over him, howling 'Johnny, oh

Johnny, don't die.' It doesn't take huge insight to realise that it is the furthest thing from her mind to comfort him, or to care for him in any way. Her aim is to show the world that she is very sad. A popular expression for this is 'Wearing your heart on your sleeve'.

It happens in rehearsals for a very good reason. After many occasions of playing a scene you realise, deep in your bones, that whether you play your action or not the other person will respond correctly. They have to. It is in the script! This makes us lazy. We lose focus on the clear task of trying to affect them, of connecting with them appropriately. We no longer play the action but rather end up giving a line reading. However, we do still want to look believable, as though we 'mean it'. So we try to *put some feeling into it.* We try to *show* the feeling.

The solution is again to go back to playing the *action* on the other person, simply, cleanly. It is early days yet and you will often find that this involvement alone is enough to allow belief in the situation to work for you again. If that doesn't happen, use a reference. You will never look fake while you are genuinely dealing with things. You will only look fake when you are posing.

Playing End Results

Closely related to showing your feelings and playing the form is the problem of arriving at new states too early. An action is played too pat, as though too assured of success. Emotional changes occur too quickly. A change of expression, a new attitude are imposed onto the face. A complex statement is understood too easily. *A new piece of information is negotiated too readily.* The most dangerous areas where this form of anticipation occurs is at 'corners'.

Indicating

This is a wonderful term which incorporates Playing the Form and Playing the Colours. The actor *indicates* what they are meant to be feeling instead of just feeling it, they indicate the action that they are meant to be playing instead of just playing it. *Indication* and *anticipation* are the two most common flaws of careless acting.

CORNERS

A *corner* is any moment which suddenly alters the direction of your character's journey, which severely alters the way in which your character was thinking or feeling, or which momentarily disorients.

(Every joke is a corner. Every surprise. Strictly speaking given that each moment is meant to be new to your character you could say that every moment should be a little corner. We will restrict ourselves to the big ones.)

I am now absolutely convinced that the most difficult aspect of preparing a performance is in identifying the corners. And then in having the courage to play them. And this is probably the most vital part of telling a story.

We have said earlier that the baby's eye has to learn where the edges are in the confusion of colours that it sees. Only after learning to identify edges can the baby perceive the shapes of the objects in the world around it. It is the same with a story. The most important aspects are the turning points, the changes of direction, the surprises. These are what give a narrative its shape. They are what the audience looks for.

The problem is that it is extremely difficult to identify corners once you have become familiar with them. Once you have read them, explored them, become acclimatised to them and have started rehearsing them it becomes very difficult to remember how unexpected they were at first meeting. The actor has the task of being very clear at every instant as to what his character might expect to happen in the next moment. When anything happens out of that expected range, that is a corner, and the character *will have to deal* with it. They will have to grapple with this moment of disorientation. This makes the most difficult demand on an actor: it requires them to pause, to stop speaking; which takes courage, faith and commitment.

BEWARE OF INSTINCTIVE TIMING

In general, an actor will listen for their word-cue, they will wait until they have heard and understood the line, and then respond. I have on occasion heard very good actors say, 'Look, my way of timing is instinctive — I don't think about it. I just respond when it *feels* right.'

This is legitimate so long as the narrative is predictable. It is a disaster when you come to a corner. Because the character cannot possibly respond to the word-cue. He or she must first deal with the disorientation. What is more is that if the character tends to not negotiate corners, the audience will, in the first instant, be a little puzzled. And finally they will lose faith in the show.

I now feel that picking up word cues is such a source of anticipation that we should probably *never* trust it. Rather we should *always* think in terms of the thought package and only respond once our character has received and understood it.

Reasons for Playing End Results

Our resistance to dealing with corners, and our tendency to play end results are simple.

1. We lose the thread of the actual internal sequence of events.

2. We believe that taking the correct time to go through the whole thought sequence will be cumbersome, pointless and ultimately boring.

3. We would like our character to look as clever and decisive as we can. We don't mind if our character seems to be able to anticipate other people and to deal with them effortlessly. (After all, if we the actor, understand the moment how come our character doesn't? We have completely forgotten how long it took for us to initially work through the intricacies of that moment.)

My crutch in understanding a moment and hence its timing centres around the following three notions:

1. what the character thinks is going to happen at that moment,

2. what actually happens, and

3. how readily the character can adjust to the difference.

Being loyal to these notions is never boring. On the contrary, they allow you to expose a real flash of your character's behaviour. What looks boring is trying to con the audience with glib, pointless authority. And do not presume that if the short cuts are played with great skill the audience won't notice. These are the same people who in real life can sense the most subtle hint of being sent-up.

When Deborah says 'I'm a Lesbian' in the David Mamet scene (described in the previous chapter) that is a severe corner for Danny. If the actor playing him ignores it, he not only robs the audience of a delicious moment, but he reminds them he knew what was coming, and that the show is a lie.

Emotional Inertia

If there is a sudden, huge explosion, of say a petrol tank in a suburb, for whole seconds afterwards absolutely nothing will happen. People will instantly freeze, and it will seem like ages before they start to move around, begin to enquire, show concern and titter. When someone tells a joke in a film or in a play, so often the director has people immediately guffaw. Not so in real life. They have to understand it first before they can deal with it.

Allow that moment of inertia to live. Trying to move people into a new emotional direction is a little like trying to crank a fly-wheel.

At first it is hard to turn, but as it gains momentum it becomes easier. If there were a second explosion then the people might scream instantly.

Any change of state takes time. It takes time to start you up, and it takes time to turn you round and it takes time to slow you down again. All timing relies on respecting these periods. But to respect them we must first realise where a start exists, where a slowing down and where a turn occurs. We must identify the corners.

There is a spectacular corner in another David Mamet play, *Speed the Plow*, which I performed in Adelaide, South Australia. It is about a couple of Hollywood film producers, low in morality and desperate for success. I played the character Fox, who has been grooming a relationship with his friend, Gould. Fox has brought Gould a product, a film, which looks as though it will put them 'up there'. It can make them very rich. The morning that he comes in to go with Gould to see the big boss to get the whole thing rolling Gould tells him that he is backing out. He has changed his mind; he doesn't want to make a moronic film that will make them enormous amounts of money, he wants to make another, more meaningful, more moral film. The audience knows that this other film is airy-fairy and a potential box-office disaster, but it was suggested to Gould by the pretty, young, idealistic secretary that he just seduced the night before.

From Fox's point of view this is devastating. If his own film doesn't get done now he has lost everything: the project, his friend, the last 11 years of nurturing him, consequently his career and his life. At the point of defeat, as he is walking out of the door, with Gould behind him saying, 'I'm sorry' Fox has an extraordinary corner. He realises that there may be a ray of hope. He has to lay bare the secretary's deepest motives to succeed. But if he can do that, if he can put her on trial, if he can prove to Gould that she herself lusts after power no less than they do, he might yet save his own life. At the door he stops, considers all of this and finally says, 'How sorry are you?' From that point on a whole new play begins — the trial of the secretary, leading to an extraordinary climax. If that point is not dealt with, if the audience does not see his life ending at that spot, then the rest of the play has no reason for being. The resolution has nothing driving it. It is redundant.

The problem is that the writer never leaves you a note in the margin saying, 'Look out for this moment. What ensues does not obviously follow what has gone before. This is a huge turning point.' It is up to the director and cast to sniff it out for themselves.

The Pause

A corner generally means a pause. In our culture there is considerable ambivalence associated with actors pausing. Here is another Dame Edith story. (I am allowed to tell it because I was Method trained.) She was rehearsing with a young 'method actor' who did nothing but pause. He would pause, presumably to motivate, before every speech … on every line … ad nauseam … During one such pause she said to him, 'Oh, do hurry dear boy. I don't have very much longer to live!'

Pausing indulgently is boring and indefensible. But to go through changes of state without taking the appropriate time is equally false, and eventually equally tedious.

> *Don't pause — let the brain go somewhere else.*

Whenever you have to pause for some reason, before or during a speech, don't let your brain stop where it is, flat footed and waiting. Take it somewhere else. The 'wedge' on page 90 is a good example.

Let us say your character cannot go on speaking. She has to pause because she is overcome with emotion. Don't fill the pause with the thought, 'I can't go on speaking.' That is obvious — you've stopped speaking. Rather fill it with 'I want to go on. I must go on. If I don't they will pick my frailty, my vulnerability.' Now you have something dynamic going on inside you. And it is probably closer to what would actually be happening to the character. It is always useful to see whether you can *fill a pause with an opposing thought*.

John Misto wrote a one man play for me called *Sky* in such a style that my character, Rocco, tells the story and yet relives the moments emotionally. At one point he is filled with terror and falls to his knees in an oil refinery, believing the flame coming out the chimney to be the devil. As he looks up at the fire he tells the audience 'I was afraid.' After loading up the fear, the silent action I played in the momentary pause before saying the line, was *to defy*. I was thinking along the lines 'Yes, I am terrified — but I am not leaving this place'. Out of that thought the admission of being afraid became more of an attempt to maintain control than to show that I was falling apart. It avoided having the line simply acknowledge the obvious.

Different is not Funny

There is a saying in the clubs that *if the band laughs at a joke during rehearsals, cut it*. Leave it out because in all likelihood the audience won't laugh. The implication is that what is funny to people who see a show night after night will not be funny to people seeing it only once.

Beware of making the cast laugh after two weeks of rehearsals. If the gag is to work for the audience it should by now be feeling very ordinary. Conversely when you change something during rehearsals, after the rest of the cast have become familiar with an older version, they may often assure you that the change is good. Don't trust them. For them different is exciting, therefore better. It may not be. Beware of their boredom.

If our little joke about Joey and the contraceptive pill (see page 5) were being rehearsed for a review, after everyone had become familiar with the puzzled delivery of 'What's a patio?' our young actor might try to liven things up at rehearsals one day by shouting the question out in desperation, as though he had asked it 30 times before. That might very well get a laugh out of the cast but it will not work for the audience. All they need to see is a little boy puzzled by the word 'patio'.

Losing sight of the actual meaning of a joke, playing end results, playing colours, playing the form are all aspects of *anticipation*. We will now consider some other guidelines to the rehearsal process.

FIGHT THE SCRIPT

We have just spoken of trying to fill a pause with an opposing thought. Earlier we said that the drunk man tries to walk straight, he does not try to stagger. These are both expressions of a very general principle. It is rare that we say things directly as they appear on paper. It is rare that the writer intended it that way. A rule of thumb is to see what will happen if you fight the script, if you try to go against the obvious meaning. Where it looks panicky see if you can control it, where it looks calm try to subdue some inner turmoil. Where it looks sincere lighten it, where it seems light give it weight. You will be surprised at how often there will turn out to be a truthful, organic reason for such inversion.

In a fifties movie, *Lonelyhearts*, Montgomery Clift is sitting on the porch telling his leading lady how embarrassing it is to talk about himself being an orphan. The young actress leans in towards him and devotedly, sincerely says to him, 'Adam, Darling. I'll be your family.' The moment hits the ground like a lump of dough. It is total, unadulterated schmaltz.

As an actor I do not regard it my job to criticise the writing. This line may not be great but it can be said, so long as the actor acknowledges the line's awkwardness. She has to somehow soften it, to go against it. One way is to include in the delivery a thought along the lines, 'Don't laugh at me as I say something as corny as this — but I can think of no other way to say it. And I do mean it.' This kind of thought is very useful for any line which feels a bit blatant, obvious, up-front.

When it comes to Shakespeare, Laurence Olivier was a master at finding readings which seem to go against the obvious meaning, yet which enrich the sense immeasurably. Here are two examples from his film of *Hamlet*. (The film is on video.)

In Act I scene 2 Horatio and Marcellus, Hamlet's friends, tell him that they saw a Ghost who looked like Hamlet's father. He was in complete battle dress including the visor. Hamlet has to ask them, 'Then saw you not his face?' (Line 229) Olivier however does not simply ask the question as though he is interested in getting the full story. He pounces on the idea that they might be wrong, that it might not be his father at all. His action is to challenge their report, to find the flaw in their argument.

Later, after Hamlet has spoken to the Ghost, he wants his two friends to swear to secrecy about the whole thing. Commenting on seeing such an apparition Horatio says, 'This is wondrous strange!' to which Hamlet says the famous line,

> There are more things in heaven and earth, Horatio,
> Than are dreamt of in your philosophy.

Again Olivier does not do the obvious, which would be to go along with the wonder of it all. Instead he uses the line to nail Horatio down, to show him how important the situation is. The line is a step towards getting them to swear to secrecy.

It is worth noting that in both these instances the manner in which Olivier distorts the meaning of the line (or enriches it) is in keeping with the overall thrust of Hamlet's intention at that point. In the first instance he would prefer that the Ghost had not been that of his father, and in the second he is intent on obtaining their pledge of secrecy.

CLARRIE — YOUR HONESTY CONSCIENCE

The $64,000 question is: how do you know whether a moment is truthful? How can we tell when it is sentimental or false or indulgent? Given that there may be a whole level of artificiality associated with style and language how can we decide on what will ring true to our audience?

This is where the clubs are an invaluable experience. Their

lesson is profound. Stand-up comedy forces you to learn the fundamentals of listening to an audience and of sensing what they are thinking. That is what tells you what they need to see at this moment in order for the next moment to work. Stand-up also teaches you simple street honesty. You cannot get up and say, 'Ladies and Gentlemen, it's great to be here with you tonight,' and sound as though you said it in the other room downstairs two hours ago. On the other hand there is no way that you can say,

> Now is the winter of our discontent
> Made glorious summer by this son of York;
> And all the clouds that lour'd upon our house
> In the deep bosom of the ocean buried.

from *Richard III* without the audience tweaking to the fact that you're acting. In a theatre people expect you to act. As a stand-up comic they expect you to talk to them and make them laugh.

I was in a production of Shakespeare's *Pericles* in England many years ago, with the Prospect Theatre Company. Near the end of the play there is a scene in which a character has to make a huge discovery (Act V, scene 3). The actress playing the role was wonderful — delicate and serene — but perhaps not with a great sense of the comical. It was a high point in the play. Pericles who believes that his wife has died at sea, is in a temple, telling his sad story to a high priestess. The priestess is in fact his wife, alive and well. She in turn thought that *he* was dead. As Pericles tells her about his drowned wife she begins to recognise him. At the end of his speech she has to say, 'Voice and favour! You are, you are — O royal Pericles! —' and faint.

What the actress did made sense. She played the peak moment of discovery right on the line 'O royal Pericles!'. And fainted. During rehearsals I remember thinking, 'This is funny'. She had this flash of discovery, and then the faint, brutally juxtaposed. I shared my concern with a chum in the cast, Ken Shorter, but of course one could not say anything. On opening night, sure enough, it got a huge laugh. The poor thing was distraught with no real idea of what she had done wrong.

We are addressing a very personal value judgment here. What is dramatically, realistically acceptable to you, and what is actually funny? Olivier has said that you can't play high tragedy unless you understand comedy. I take that to mean that unless you understand how to break the tension to get a laugh you won't know how to maintain the tension in a dramatic moment.

As I say, what is funny and what isn't, what is honest and what isn't are very personal value judgments. They are also very culture specific, but in our communities this following notion might help.

There was a stage of adolescence when you realised that your parents were fallible; when you discovered hypocrisy and hated it; when you were surprised to find that social mores were ultimately arbitrary. It was a time when ideals were clear, when your sense of truth was obvious, when you knew what was right and wrong and when you discovered cynicism. It was around this time you saw the lie in the theatre performances on school outings and rolled Jaffas down the aisle. This anarchist, this rebel, this street-wise urchin is still inside you now. I will call it Clarrie — short for Clarity. This unpretentious critic is your most valuable guide towards naiveté, honesty and the common touch. When in doubt ask Clarrie. Would she think this moment was dramatic or funny? Would she be convinced or bored?

Had the Shakespearian actress in *Pericles* been able to ask these questions she might have played the real recognition of Pericles during *his* speech. By the time she spoke, her action would then have been something like 'to grapple with the possibility that this was him', 'to fight against the doubt', 'to affirm'. Never something as blatant as 'to discover', or 'to celebrate'! It would have made her line softer. It would have allowed the audience to recognise her dilemma, to let them sense her enormous emotional turmoil and precarious inner state. By the time she fainted they would have been ready for it.

To kill a laugh warn the audience of the switch; tip them off. To stay linked with them create a need for the next moment. Unfortunately she did neither. She gave them someone greatly surprised, and then someone on the floor. A shock at a tense moment. Tension and surprise — a very dangerous mixture. They responded as the Clarries within their own bosoms dictated — by laughing. Clarrie is ruthless. But invaluable.

CREATE THE NEED FOR THE NEXT MOMENT

One of the most powerful elements of good story telling is to create a need for the next moment. In the most general sense this means making the audience aware of a building emotion in the character which will justify what he or she is about to do, or generating a growing need in the audience for a particular event to take place.

Shakespeare himself uses this device constantly in the

construction of his plays. He wants to start *Hamlet* by having the Ghost tell Hamlet of his father's murder. He does not, however have Hamlet discovered sitting on the stage and the Ghost coming on and telling him the plot. No. In scene 1 we have the soldiers see the Ghost, in scene 2 they tell Hamlet about it, in scene 4 Hamlet sees the Ghost which beckons to him, and in scene 5 it finally tells him the story. By this time the audience is dying to know it too.

If you do get the video of Olivier's *Hamlet* you will see dozens of instances where Olivier applies this principle, both as a director and as an actor. In the last scene Gertrude, Hamlet's mother, has drunk the poisoned wine meant for Hamlet. In this interpretation she deliberately drinks it, presumably to save Hamlet's life. We then see a series of stages of the poison taking its effect on her, but nobody else notices. Hamlet and Laertes meanwhile have both been scratched by a poison-tipped sword. There is a wonderful moment when in the foreground we see Gertrude slumping over in her chair, while in the background all attention is on Laertes lying on the floor. But Hamlet alone is looking our way and sees the queen slumping over. There is dialogue asking Laertes how he is, and a line from Horatio asking Hamlet how he is, before Hamlet finally says, 'How does the queen?' and rushes over to her. By this time the viewer is in agony wanting to have the poor queen looked after.

PLOT THE JOURNEY

In the last chapter we discussed how useful it was to understand the spine of your character, and what he was trying to achieve in each scene and how all these scenes added up to your character's journey through the play. That was an overview of your character's life in terms of *intentions* — the solid ground of what it is that your character is trying to achieve throughout the course of the show.

It is now equally necessary to gain a clear picture of your character's *emotional* journey through the course of the play or film. By this I mean decide at which point the character hits his deepest low, where is his moment of greatest joy, where is he most torn by indecision and where is his most violent rage. Thereafter keep an eye out on all other similar moments and make sure that none compete. No depression can be as low as the lowest, and no rage as great as the highest. Rather let all others lead to and support these pinnacles and troughs. Above all identify where the main dilemma occurs. Which is *the* crisis point for your character? And design your performance to build towards that, to support that. Let no other crisis overshadow it.

By visualising the shape of your character's life through the progression of the story you will avoid repetition. What at first appear to be similar moments will be seen to have quite different functions, different content.

Ignoring this overview leaves you in danger of repeating the same scene over and over. If, in the playing, several scenes have the same emotional journey, if they look the same and feel the same, then their sum total will lead nowhere. And when you do arrive at the critical moment of your performance you will find members of the audience looking at their watches.

GENERAL PRINCIPLES FOR REHEARSALS

WRITTEN FOR *YOU*

No matter who else has played your role before, if possible approach it as though it had been specifically written for you. This will allow you to think in terms of what the writer would have wanted *you* to do, given your personality, your range, your type of skills. It will make your responses to the script more personal. It will help you colour the character with your own soul.

BAD COVER* — GOOD CHARACTER

Where possible find the quirks in your character. There is nothing very interesting about a character with a perfect cover. Watch people who find it difficult to communicate, who find it difficult to maintain eye contact, or to appear honest. Awkward, pretentious, pompous, elusive, sleazy, flawed people are what give society its colour. Smooth, bland and well adjusted are the ways that we have visualised our heroes, but as characters these do tend to be forgettable. I believe that Dustin Hoffman was originally offered the 'nice' role in the film *Midnight Cowboy* but that he held out for the sick, ugly, sleazy, delicious role of Ratso Rizzo. We can't all play the Ratsos of the world but a hero will always be made more interesting if there are little chinks, little flaws in the make-up.

WHERE POSSIBLE ANTICIPATE THE OPPOSITE.

Whenever there is a choice between your character knowing what is coming next, and not knowing, there are good arguments for

---

* All of us, to a greater or lesser extent, play a character in real life, which is our 'social self', the character we present to the outside world. This is what I call our 'cover'. Some might call it our persona. It is the set of behaviour we have evolved through life to interact with our social surroundings. Some people are comfortable with their covers, others are not.

choosing the latter. It makes it so much easier to not anticipate. The more you can decoy yourself the easier it will be to trick the audience.

> ### KEEP IT ROUGH
> As we do a thing over and over we naturally find the easiest, simplest, neatest way of doing it. Rehearsals smooth out behaviour. Real life is rough, we fumble, we make mistakes. When acting you are supposed to be doing that move for the first time, not the thirtieth. Keep the roughness. Don't iron it out with practice. Don't work out too well how to pick up the bag, umbrella and raincoat at the door when leaving.

The Wedge

When you become too familiar with a series of events and find it difficult not to anticipate the next moment a solution is to throw in an extra thought, in keeping with the kind of thing that the character would be likely to think. Such a thought I call a wedge.

Let us say that the other person has to say 'You're an idiot.' and you have to answer, 'What?'

And let us assume that the director does not want it to be a simple question — 'What did you say?' but rather a surprise. He wants a little stunned pause, as if to say 'I don't believe I heard that. What did he say?' before your question. The 'what' would then become something like to double check, or to probe, to get your bearings.

At first that stunned moment will be easy to play. But after a few rehearsals you might find that the pause has become awkward and empty, little more than a hold-up in your performance. You really would rather just drop it and get on with the show, but the director insists that he needs it for punctuation. My solution is to fill the pause with something else.

After 'You're an idiot.' think something like 'How dare he?' and prepare to say 'I'm not an idiot.' Prepare to stand your ground, prepare to challenge the other person. As soon as that notion has formed, drop out of it all together and do a whole new start to the conversation with the scripted question, 'What?'.

The 'wedge' is the preparation to rebuff the other character. To then stop that development and return to the scripted enquiry, 'What?' is difficult. The effort required to execute such a switch looks similar to what happens to you when you really are disoriented. No doubt there are similarities between the mental processes of regaining your balance and changing direction. But in any case the pause of indecision will stay alive if you fill it with a silent action which is then abandoned.

When you put in the wedge it does not mean that you pull faces, or mouth imaginary words, or indicate the thoughts. And it need not take two weeks. It only needs the nimbleness to think the thought crisply and deliberately. Such a sequence will give you both the disorientation and subsequent loading that you need.

Paragraph Acting

Paragraph acting is waiting for the other person to do their whole speech so that you can come in with your own. You do not listen to them so much as wait for them. You know the end result of their speech because you have heard it 30 times before, so you prepare yourself to respond *to that final moment,* before they have even started.

This is dead acting. It is flat-footed. You are robbing yourself of the opportunity of tracking their argument, and of responding to the twists and turns of their speech, which would give your character life.

The solution is to:

• Be clear as to what your character feels about what the other person is saying at each point.

• Be prepared, at every instant, to do whatever your character would do if the other person were to suddenly stop speaking.

• Be aware of where your character thinks the other person is heading at any moment.

• Be very clear about where in the other person's speech your character has understood the point that you are about to address with your next speech.

Paragraph acting is also when *you* deliver a long speech as though it were one solid lump. Remember that your character has no idea at the beginning of the speech of exactly how she is going to say it. It evolves as she progresses. And as mentioned earlier, if your character had achieved what she wanted after the first sentence she would not have gone on. Every moment in a long speech is trying to complete what has been left undone by the previous section. That does not mean that the speech moves in a straight line. It tortures and twists its way to completion, but it does so at each point because the character feels that something has been left undone.

The simple rules are:

- *Play the moment, not the paragraph.*
- *Respond to the moment, not to the paragraph.*

Dare to Prepare Very, Very Late

You may have realised by now that what we are really fighting is early preparation. As novices we would prepare very early indeed. The other actor started to speak and we were ready with our next line, attitude and gestures intact, ready to go. We weren't going to be caught unprepared, no way!

But, ultimately, you will have to learn to leave preparation insanely late. It will take courage to wait beyond the moment of no return, beyond the point where you actually have *time* to prepare. But that is what you must do if you are ever to give a semblance of a living moment. Because only in this way will you be able to take in and respond to the very latest things that are happening in your fellows actor's eyes, and in the audience's hearts. You cannot time a comedy moment in advance. It depends on how the audience feels at this split second.

Be a Moron

It was while watching the 1980 Wimbledon final between Bjorn Borg and John McEnroe that the simple solution of how to prepare so late came to me. I know the point I am about to make is about as original as the twittering of the birds, but it is a discovery that needs to be made personally and graphically. There was a point in the match when Borg was down 0–40. As often happens when champions are under extreme pressure a shadow glided over him and his manner somehow changed ever so slightly. It was as though he had changed gear; clicked into a slightly higher level of concentration.

From here on he could only be described as seeming to be stupid; unaware of the score, of where he was, or of what was at stake. All he now focussed on was the ball. This ball now in the air. He did what he could to get this one back. And then the next. And the next. He won the point, the set and finally the match. And I remember thinking, 'That's it! That is the secret of acting. Be a moron. Do not think into the future. Just play this ball now. This moment.' As I say, hardly original, but very useful.

I have mentioned Timothy Gallwey and his book *The Inner Game* (page 65), and his concept of the two selves: Self 1, the judge, critic, analyser, and Self 2, the doer, the intuitive performer. I think that these two characters apply equally well to acting. Self 1 senses the audience, and guides the whole operation. But Self 2 is well served to be stupid. To not share in the overview; to focus simply on this moment. *It is only by focussing on this moment that we can blind ourselves to the next one.* That is how we can dare to crash into the imaginary brick wall of the play's future.

GO BEFORE READY

Once you have loaded up emotionally, don't over-prepare the moment you are about to play. However you think of acting, whether in terms of the line you are about to say, or the thought you are about to send, or the action you are about to play, *before it is fully formed, start playing it*. Let your playing of it give it its final definition. If you think it through completely and then start playing, it will feel like an echo. I stress I am not talking about your *reference* not being ready. Your emotional loading should be complete, but not your image of what you are about to *do*. Starting off-balance is a wonderful way of keeping the moment fresh and dangerous.

EMOTIONS COME IN WAVES

High emotions tend to manifest themselves in bursts. Extreme rage or intense weeping are rarely continuous activities. They seem to come in waves. After each outburst the energy seems to be spent and needs to be recharged. There will be a moment of respite, a lull, during which time the anger or sorrow will rebuild and then be let out in the next outburst. There is nothing more exciting than for the audience to see the contrast and share that ominous lull.

LET THE MOMENT GO

As important as creating the moment is the ability to let it go. Somehow this might be one of the single most salient requirements in all of acting — knowing when a moment is over. From this knowledge all else follows. It is at the heart of all timing. And once it is over do not try to hang onto it. You won't make it more poignant. Have the courage to let it go and to embrace the next moment.

REMEMBER THE FLOOR

One of the finest actors that I have ever worked with is David Warner. He played Claudius in Tony Richardson's production of *I Claudius* at the Queens Theatre, London, 1972. This was an adaptation by John Mortimer of the Robert Graves books *I Claudius* and *Claudius the God*.

There was a moment when we senators were all gathered round

a model of the proposed new docks of Rome, kneeling or squatting. As Warner, playing the stuttering emperor, was looking at the model another actor came in and said to him something like, 'We don't want the workers to go on strike as a result of us changing the docks.' To which Warner had to say, 'No. No, we don't want that.'

I was a young actor then, recently arrived from Australia. My tendency in that moment would have been to act a lot; showing the importance of this line, the gravity of the situation, and of the model before us, and of my role, etc., etc. I was therefore astounded during rehearsals when I saw David, squatting to my left, look at the model, and look at the *floor boards*, and do absolutely nothing.

He stopped 'acting'. He had no overt expression. He seemed to have dropped out of the scene, waiting for something, before suddenly remembering his friend. He looked up at him and said, 'No. No, we don't want that.' To me the moment was absolutely riveting. Because it was so dangerous. And so natural.

Later in front of the audience it became astonishing, because here was a moment of absolute rest, against which the audience could measure the rest of the performance. It gave it a base line, a criterion for truth. All he did was look at the floor boards.

I mention it because every now and then, at a well chosen moment, it is very useful to drop your performance, drop your character, drop the show; give your audience that dangerous moment of relief. Sometimes you will find that it can actually come in the lull between two peaks of rage or anguish. Then its effect is extraordinary. Remember the floor.

You Block on a Real Problem

It sometimes happens in rehearsals that an actor can never remember a particular line. Every time they come to it they seize up. It is frightening when it happens to you. But there is a way of dealing with it. It is based on the idea that the line you block on reminds you of some real, unresolved problem in your life. It might be a current issue, or a distant childhood anxiety. But either way, the assumption is that the line subconsciously reminds you of something painful, and your defence mechanisms protect you from the pain by stopping you from remembering it.

Like with dreams, the association might be symbolic, or hidden in a double meaning. Bear with my amateur psychology for a moment. It works — but for the wrong reasons!

Dig deep into yourself until you have found a possible association with the maverick line. Be as honest as you can. Here is why. Whether or not you have correctly identified your reason for drying, by now you have focussed on the line so intensely, you have inspected it so thoroughly and linked it to such powerful references, that you will never again forget it. It works.

THE MORE YOU CRY THE EASIER IT GETS

Like golf or snooker the more you practise the easier crying gets. When the lump forms in your throat and the eyes redden while watching a movie, don't fight it, let it happen. Allow the mechanisms to be well oiled, to have had plenty of use. Practice also helps laughing. If you rarely laugh, it will be very difficult for you to do it on stage.

TRAVEL LIGHT

Having said to keep it rough, throw in a wedge, observe the corners, dare to go up the blind alleys, all of which are devices which help us reproduce the living activity, I will now say 'keep it simple'.

By the time the show opens you will have a good idea of all the idiosyncrasies of your characterisation, and the roughness necessary to simulate this life. Now I say: leave it alone. Be very wary of cluttering any moment for the sake of 'art'. No piece of business, no gesture, no inflection should be there merely because it is 'interesting'. If it does not serve to convey clearly what is absolutely necessary, my preference is — leave it out. 'Art is the science of omission.' (I don't know who said that.)

SUMMARY

1. Go through all the thoughts necessary for a particular process to occur.

2. Stay alert, listen, take in everything that is happening around you.

3. Beware of the 'obvious' reading. Soften it, harden it, be guided by Clarrie. Do what the writer meant, not what they wrote.

4. Find good strong references whenever necessary.

5. Anticipate what your character *thinks* is going to happen. He or she has not read the script.

6. Dare to prepare the next beat as late as your courage will allow. You may want to do a quick check of what the beginning of your next line is. Apart from that, follow your character's thoughts and misassumptions until the actual moment that your character would understand the cue. Aim to start preparing the next moment as late as your character would. It is impossible, but that is utopia.

7. Don't presume that your action will be successful. Play it totally, then see how you went. Follow it through. Check the object.

8. Dare to slam into the mental brick walls of the future. Dare to take the sharpest corners possible in your journey. Blind yourself to the next moment of time by focussing totally on the present one.

9. When a moment is over, let it go.

10
CHARACTERISATION

I have mentioned children learning behaviour by imitating adults, for example, me rocking on the balls of my feet at age 5, or a little girl with her hands on her hips imitating her mother's long-suffering pose. I suggest that the mechanisms we used in order to carry out these imitations are at the heart of what we do as actors in generating characterisations. We have all been there, trying to match an image in our minds with a piece of behaviour we perform. Most fundamental for me however is the following observation.

KEVIN COSTNER

My sons taped a programme in which Ray Martin interviewed Kevin Costner. I was working in another room when my sons and my wife started watching it. Suddenly they rushed in and said I had to come out and see this. The excitement centred around the fact that Costner was looking ordinary, he was not recognisable as his usual glamorous self. What was he doing? What had happened?

The object lesson was invaluable. Through the interview there were snippets from Costner's various films, so we had instant contrasts between him at work, and him here being interviewed. Without any visible changes in his adjustments, same voice, same physical characteristics, we saw two distinct human beings. This rarely happens with Hollywood stars because so often they carry their screen personae over into the interview situation. Here we had a man who has obviously tried to retain some semblance of his pre-Hollywood humanness and was showing it here in this interview.

Put very simply, as the hero, Costner would play actions like: to impose upon, to control, to challenge, to dominate, to take on, to assure, to assert, to brush off, to brood. As himself, he played actions like: to accommodate, to open himself up, to share his frailties, to reason, to consider, to squirm, to wheedle, to edge sideways, to acknowledge, to fraternise, to justify, to complain. It was a magnificent example, showing how totally a person's character can change purely by altering the kinds of actions he is playing.

Spencer Tracy

Tracy was a master at this. There is very little difference in his adjustments between *Judgment at Nüremberg* and *The Broken Lance*. The voice, the look, the walk are unchanged. But the attitudes, the interactions with others, his soul if you like, are totally different. It again rests on his choice of actions. As the innocent outsider, the American lawyer becoming aware of the horrors of the Holocaust in *Nüremberg*, Tracy plays a lot of weighing up, considering, feeling out, analysing and sympathising kinds of actions. His tough, less educated, self-made rancher in *Broken Lance* on the other hand, bulldozes and challenges and blusters his way through life. This is my favourite form of characterisation: where you do change the *soul*, but the audience is hard pressed to see what it is that you have done.

When the changes in attitude and actions are backed up by well-observed changes in voice and movement, and topped off with clever make-up, then the result can be breathtaking.

ANALYSIS

Mimics and impersonators can systematically analyse and dismantle another person's way of speaking or walking and reassemble it in themselves. They will observe the speech patterns, intonations, vowel sounds and consonants; they will study the walk and gestures, adopt these characteristics and end up with a very clever representation of that person. Although the character actor is frequently called upon to enter this arena it is a specialised one and does not need to be discussed in detail here.

I am more interested to look at short cuts; some of the little games, tricks and tips that do result in astonishing leaps into characterisation. The key to successful imitation of course is painstaking observation.

OBSERVATION

Here are a couple of simple examples.

I know a man whose right toe is turned in and whose right knee is permanently bent when he walks. Having told you this, you can immediately adopt a walk which will begin to resemble his. As your imitation became more refined you would need to observe him directly for a clearer notion of how he shifts his balance and how the rest of his body compensates for his disability when he moves. But the first step is always to observe the walk and to come to a simple understanding of how the disability manifests itself.

My own mother is very old and often short of breath. It appears that when she breathes in, she is not able to take in as much air as she would like, and when she breathes out she has to force it slightly as though there were some obstruction. To simply say that she is short of breath does not tell you how to do it. Once you break it down into simple elements, and project onto her what you think she is feeling, it becomes easier. A shallow breath in, and then a gentle push out of the air. The hardest part is the analysis.

Underlying this form of deliberate analysis is what we did as children. It was a disorganised, generalised form of imitation, where we almost breathed in the subtle cues by osmosis. To some extent we do this throughout life. Watch a person promoted in their job. Within a matter of months their ways of interacting with their colleagues will have begun to subtly adjust, in a direction demanded by the new position. It is unlikely that much of that change would have come from conscious observation.

> ### EXERCISE: Pull a Face
> Here is a silly little exercise. For many years I have amused myself by seizing on a particularly rich expression in a passer-by and, after they have walked past me, imitating it. No thought, no analysis, just whack it on — pull the face. It is wonderful practice to try to express what they seem to *feel*. It sounds insane I know. Just make sure that there is no one in front of you to see you doing it. You can feel stupid! Remember, put on the face that results from what they seemed to be feeling or thinking at that instant. Try to let yourself feel and think those things as you do it. (This is not what you do when performing! This is a loosening up exercise, it is an exercise in projection.)

PROJECTION

A great deal of this work hinges on 'projection'. In this context it means projecting onto the other person what we *think* they are feeling. This need have little to do with what they are in fact feeling. But it is a great help to latch onto such an assumed emotion when imitating. We do the same with animals. We see the look of the camel and call it arrogant. This helps us put on that expression. (For all we know the camel might in fact be quite humble.)

When applied to imitating another person's walk or speech, projection becomes invaluable.

One asks: what would it feel like to be making that sound? To be moving like that? How does a particular impediment feel? How does the moment feel as the stutterer is fighting his inner resistance? By believably finding such a resistance within yourself, and then trying to deal with it, you will give a good imitation of the stutter. The stutterer does not try to stop, he tries to speak.

We have a neutral vowel sound in English, for example, the 'a' in 'around', or the 'e' in 'velocity'. It is little more than a gentle grunt. Just a catch of sound. An Italian will try to go smoothly from the word 'some' to the word 'thing' when he says 'something'. But there is a catch. From the sounds that he has learnt and spoken all his life there is a break, a discontinuity which he is forced to negotiate between the 'm' and the 'th'. It is little more than the neutral hesitation mentioned above. He does not try to say (as the cliché imitation would have it) 'some-a-thing'. But there is that subtle, neutral intrusion there. If you can impose for yourself the feeling of that momentary barrier then your attempt to overcome it is what will give you a plausible Italian sound.

> **EXERCISE: DO A RELATIVE**
> Think of someone very close to you, a parent or relative. Choose someone with interesting idiosyncrasies — a distinctive way of expressing themselves, of gesturing, walking or talking. Now take a nursery rhyme that you know very well, or three or four lines of a song or poem — say Twinkle Twinkle Little Star — and recite it in the manner that this person would *normally converse with you*. Use their attitudes, gestures and pauses. I think you will be surprised.
>
> I have seen the most inhibited people become liberated. Shy, awkward, conservative people, who think they can't 'do characters' get up and behave in the most extraordinary ways. They create rich, subtle, imaginative characters. Of course they don't think that they are 'creating' them. They feel that they are merely copying a real entity that is inside them, that they know well. They will rarely feel that their characterisation is perfect but they invariably achieve a behaviour surprisingly different from their own. The beauty of this exercise is that very little attention is placed on the mannerisms themselves. Most of the attention stays on the actions that their role model would play, making the characterisation look effortless, rounded, resonant.

THE INNER EYE

The instrument we use to view these internal images of our relatives I call the Inner Eye. You use it when telling a story, for example about someone who in your opinion 'thinks they're smart' and you momentarily put on their haughty expression as you talk. When you do these impersonations there is no analysis. You do not think of what you need to alter in yourself in order to do them. You follow a vision which exists inside you and which you can somehow translate directly into caricature. I feel that we are dealing here with mechanisms that date back to childhood.

Your Inner Eye has images of all your friends, acquaintances, aunts, uncles and teachers. When you begin to read a script, a few of these people will begin to float to the surface of your consciousness, and what you will end up playing will often be a deliberate cocktail of two or three of them.

ANIMAL IMAGERY

The Inner Eye has a host of other entities it can conjure up, for example animals. A powerful technique for characterisation is to use the concept of a particular animal. If the role is a big, lumbering person we might think of a bear; if light and quick, we might use the image of a sparrow. We call this Animal Imagery. Its power is that the mere thought of the animal will immediately affect your attitude. It can instantly influence the physical life of your character. The degree to which you play the animal is up to you. You may want to incorporate into your performance characteristics so specific that even the audience can pick what animal you are playing. (His head movements are a bit like a hen. Isn't she like a snake?) Or you may want to use only the subtlest of tinges.

In general, millions of forms of imagery are possible. Imagine your head getting light, and gently lifting up, lifting off your shoulders. Imagine a vertical rod forming in your back and straightening your spine, lifting your chest.

See how susceptible we are?

THE ENERGY CENTRE

A very simple and powerful device to alter the way you walk is to toy with the notion: which part of the body is driving you forward? Where is the Energy Centre of the movement? This is a very evocative concept. Above I asked you to lighten your head, to let it float upwards, off your shoulders. I will now ask you to let your nose lead your head forward gently, as you are sitting here. Now imagine walking, being led by your nose. In fact if space and present company permit, get up and try it. Walk around being led by your nose.

Now imagine your toes as the Energy Centre of your walk. You are being drawn forward by your toes. Try it. See what happens. You can try walking with your chest leading you. Imagine that an invisible string is pulling you forward by your chest. Then your navel. Then your forehead.

You will see that such a simple concept as the Energy Centre can make an immediate and effortless change to the way you move.

Conversely, when analysing a walk it is often useful to try to identify where the Energy Centre seems to be. For example, the awkward stumble of a toddler could be described as having the Energy Centre in the knees. But they are being drawn upwards rather than forwards. (In order not to trip, the child may well be more preoccupied, at this stage, with getting its feet off the ground than with advancing.)

A tantalising observation occurred in a class I was giving: leading with the *buttocks* results in a very good likeness of the waddle of a pregnant woman. Move as though your bottom is being gently pushed forward from behind, don't take very big steps, and you have a very good first approximation to a difficult adjustment.

AVOID STOCK CHARACTERS

When we talk about concepts like the Inner Eye and the Energy Centre there is a danger of looking for a 'formula' with which to play a character. There is always a danger that we will fall into the trap of playing a cliché. The techniques are useful as exercises, and at most as a starting point for a characterisation. But by themselves, without thorough research, they are useless, they are mere generalisations.

At kindergarten I remember being shown how to draw a tree — two parallel vertical lines, topped by a circle. I have looked for such a tree long and hard. It does not exist.

The trees that I do see have so much more character, detail and beauty.

I once heard an experienced colleague say, 'All you need to play a Russian is to lower your voice and roll the r's.' He was serious.

Actors called upon to play a character from a class or ethnic group other than their own will often lean towards a predetermined characterisation, a stock set of tricks that they have either played before or seen someone else play. Far better to change your circle of friends for a while. Get to know people from the character's social group and see society through their eyes. You will discover a whole range of possibilities for your character, far more original, and far more vibrant. In other words have a look at a real tree and draw that.

Princess Margaret's ex-husband, Antony Armstrong-Jones, a very successful photographer, was once quoted as saying 'As I get older, more and more often I find that I rely on experience when at one time only inspiration would have sufficed.'

When approaching a new production you have the opportunity to create the role from scratch, to do fresh research, appropriate to this writer, this director, this production. If you bring in your tired old tricks you will only blur what is precious within you. The audience has not come to see tricks, they have come to view souls; to connect with some aspect of the humanity within you. I suggest that you do not put on a characterisation to *hide* your soul but rather to expose a part of it more clearly.

> ## PERSONALITY ACTORS
> There is a group of actors of course, indeed amongst the most successful, who seem to play the same character all the time. The film stars. You hear people say, 'Oh, he can't act. He's always the same in everything he does.' Amongst my own favourites are Spencer Tracy, Katharine Hepburn, James Stewart, Robert Mitchum, Ingrid Bergman — always believable, always enthralling, always the same. (Well, almost.)
>
> England constantly has a clutch of brilliant character actors who have developed one primary persona: John Le Mesurier, Arthur Lowe (both in *Dad's Army*) and Leo McKern (*Rumpole of the Bailey*).
>
> You might ask, 'How come we don't mind seeing *their* tricks over and over?' The answer is that they are not tricks. These actors have worked-in a set of adjustments which they use over and over. The illusion is that they are merely 'playing themselves'. But of course they are not. They play an invention, a character which is related to some ideal, or essential aspect of themselves, and they learn to perfect that through the course of their careers. And because these characters, in some sense, satisfy or excite an audience, or symbolise a whole character type, they are very useful.
>
> I would suggest that the reason we don't get bored with the same mannerisms here is because they have arisen out of these actors' own beings, they were not imposed from the outside. Being extensions of real characteristics they tend to be original, detailed and very complex. Also, because they are so well worked-in, they require almost no attention and look absolutely natural. From below their elaborate quirks and idiosyncrasies the souls of James Stewart and Katharine Hepburn always shone through.

TRY TO PLAY AGAINST TYPE

The golden rule appears here again, this time in a much broader context: the drunk man tries to walk straight. If you are playing a good person, a person who does kind things, you can often afford to have him seem rude. He knows he is good. He does not have to protest it to the world. In fact if you play a good person nicely you are likely to end up with treacle. Spencer Tracy spent his life playing gruff saints. The principle is supported by real life. In his everyday interactions Dr Fred Hollows was apparently a very rough diamond, the same apparently is true of Mother Teresa. On the other hand conmen, thieves and criminals have very good reason to present themselves as charmingly as possible. The most sincere, concerned, gentle and self-justified people I have ever seen on television have been hardened criminals in gaol being interviewed. So, when playing a bad person see if there is room for playing him nicely. Lee Strasberg used this beautifully in *The Godfather II*. I certainly based the whole character of Robert, in *Mother and Son*, on this principle. Robert has to believe that he is a nice guy or there is no comedy.

Providing this opposite dimension will generally add a depth to your character, a roundness. It will also create a tension between what he is and what he presents to the world.

LIFE-CUES

Throughout our behaviour we have tiny little quirks and mannerisms — little shrugs and sighs, intimate glances, an understanding nod, a half-muttered grunt. They are common to all cultures. It is not too much to say that these are the most powerful link that we have with one another's humanity. Whether we are watching a group of Kalahari Bushmen conferring in a television documentary, or seeing a group of Japanese businessmen in a restaurant, it is these tiny, universal cues, which allow us to recognise them, to feel connected to them. I call these life-cues.

Even when a dog sighs, we smile in recognition. Life-cues are the most powerful link that we have with the audience. They will recognise them instantly, identify with them and feel comforted.

Life-cues are the first things we omit when we try to adopt a character that we don't know very well, because a few weeks, or even months, of research are not enough to tell us which kind of look away or shrug is appropriate in a particular interaction. We don't want to contaminate our new character with our own life-cues so we do nothing. Consequently shallow characterisations, such as you see on daytime television soaps, tend to have few life-cues, while personality performances abound with them. One looks bland, the other reeks of life. It is a question of familiarity and honesty. Notice that when a good actor, whose parents are of a different culture, plays a character of that culture, again all those tiny cues tend to be delightfully present, intact and twinkling.

CHARACTERISATION

ADJUSTMENTS ARE NOT FREE — TRAVEL LIGHT

Big adjustments do demand some attention. No matter how well you work them in there is always some small attention that heavy adjustments will demand of you while acting. That amount of attention will not then be available for other things, such as instantaneous alertness to the other actor's behaviour.

Also, new adjustments can interfere with your own life-cues. As mentioned above a heavy characterisation can inhibit spontaneous use of your own life-cues. You will not be sure what flickers your character would actually have at this moment.

For these two reasons my advice is: *Travel Light*.

Make the characterisation as economical as possible. Certainly you want the audience to have no difficulty in believing that you are who you are meant to be. Beyond that leave the characterisation as light as possible. Give yourself the option, that when in doubt as to what the *character* would do, you can make a sensitive guess and use life-cues from your own repertoire. Allow some of your own living elements to seep through.

YOU ARE WHAT YOU ARE CHANGING

This leads me to a simple but important notion. *The entity you are altering in order to create the new character is yourself, no one else.* Always remember that your own being is the base line of any characterisation you adopt. In other words, at those moments when you and the character you are playing have an attribute in common *you don't need to change anything*. It may seem ludicrous to point this out but there is good reason. In the case of adopting an accent, for example, once an actor is in the mode of 'I must now put on this strange accent' there is a tendency to produce only sounds which feel alien — even when the sound required is identical to the way the actor normally speaks. The trick is to stay very alert to what you and the character have in common and, once identified, leave it alone! Allow your own self to seep through. This applies to the way your character walks and to their mannerisms. In general terms, the humanity that you are portraying is yours as well as your character's. Let it seep through.

A variation of this theme is:

Don't go out to the character, bring the character home to you.

Every human being has his or her limits of versatility and flexibility. However talented and experienced the performer there are things that he or she cannot do comfortably. There is then a danger when trying to give an exact rendition of the character that you lose your own centre; that you feel as though you are going out to the character. Don't. Try to think of bringing the character home to you. If you are comfortable in your characterisation the audience will believe it. If not, they won't. At the risk of raising a few eyebrows I will come straight out and say it:

It is worse to try to play an ideal characterisation awkwardly, than to play a slightly wrong character comfortably.

It is undoubtedly the artist's responsibility to constantly explore and stretch herself with every role. But new skills should be drilled in the rehearsal room and in classes, not on stage. For art to be effective it must appear effortless.

PLAY THE COVER

I have often found it liberating to tell myself that all we ever see of a human is their façade, what they present to the outside world. We never see their inner selves directly. Consequently:

You only ever have to play the character's cover, you never really have to play the character.

I'll try to explain what I mean. When you try to 'play the character' you try to imagine what the character feels and respond accordingly. When you 'play the character's *cover*' you present a lie. It is the outward appearance that the character presents to the world and not an honest expression of what they feel. This gives the actor greater freedom because it acknowledges that real life is a lie. We all have a cover, and in many instances that cover is not very good, it is often clumsy, awkward. A character approached in this way can be terribly effective.

An example for me was Tom Hanks as Forrest Gump. The girl that he has idolised and wanted to marry throughout the film comes back one day and says to him, 'Will you marry me, Forrest?' Hanks goes through the elation and the astonishment. But when it finally comes to say the line 'OK', his action is to casually grant, to do her a small favour. It is totally subdued. Forrest won't let her see the ecstasy and upheaval going on inside. The actor loads up for real, but then only plays the cover.

PLAY THE CHARACTER FROM INSIDE OR OUTSIDE?

I will end this chapter with a subject which goes to the very heart of what it is that we are trying to do as actors. The question asked is: Are you inviting the audience to simply observe your character, or do you want them to live the story through the character's brain?

I have seen actors give performances which were well observed, accurately executed, which were engrossing and captivating, but with which we did not really empathise. Laurence Olivier in the film *Wuthering Heights* gives a riveting performance as Heathcliff, but he seems to stand outside the character. It is as though he were presenting him to us, saying 'Watch this character. Observe how I'm depicting him.' The result is that in the film we do not empathise with Heathcliff, yet in the novel he is very moving.

In the same year, Charles Laughton played *The Hunchback of Notre Dame*. His make-up was grotesque. His walk and speech were distorted to the point where he seemed barely human. Yet Laughton managed to let us suffer with Quasimodo. He dragged us into his perception and made us feel the world through his heart.

The distinction between the two approaches is subjective — one person will be utterly moved by a performance while another person is not. It is elusive to try to pin-down how they differ. But one does seem to play the character from outside, the other from inside.

It seems to me that the difference can again be expressed in terms of timing — the time taken for emotions to establish and for decisions to be made.

When playing from outside, you time the way you imagine the character would. When playing from inside, you time as though *you* would, if you were the character (as if the character's internal processes were happening inside you).

The former is taken from an external perception of how someone might behave, and an attempt to reproduce that. The latter is guided by your own empathy with the character — your projection of what he or she might feel — your own sense of how long those processes would take in you. In genuinely going through those thoughts and emotions I think you cause the audience to go through them with you.

> There are times, however, when playing from outside is absolutely the right thing to do. I will use two of my very dear friends as examples here — Warren Mitchell and Leo McKern. Warren chose to play Alf Garnett from outside with spectacularly good effect. He wanted the audience to say, 'Yes Warren, you are right. Alf is a fool.' Leo, on the other hand, played Rumpole from inside, with equally brilliant effect. His aim was for the audience to see only one entity, to see the stories through the McKern/Rumpole mind.

SUMMARY
1. Actions alone can change you.
2. There are many clear and useful tricks for adopting characteristics. Animal Imagery, the Energy Centre.
3. The major part of imitation is correct *observation*.
4. Travel light. Use only the adjustments that are necessary. Don't weigh yourself down with too heavy a characterisation:
   a. to remain flexible and alert.
   b. to bring the character to you — to remain comfortable.
   c. to allow yourself to use some of your own life-cues and so to allow aspects of your own soul to shine through.

11
MEET THE AUDIENCE

To me the first contact with the audience contains the most exhilarating moments in all of acting. After weeks, sometimes months of preparation, long after we have lost any kind of objective view of the play, after every moment has acquired a rehearsal/drill familiarity, to suddenly have outside brains see the event, share it; to have our carefully fashioned moments explode in their minds, suddenly reminds us of what it was all about. The moments are instantly reborn through the perception of other people. It is divine.

FILM AND TELEVISION
In film and television of course we never have this luxury. The actor ends up putting on the screen what you might call the last full-dress rehearsal. It can often be a more spontaneous, internal and intimate process but the performance never connects with an audience. It is up to the director, there and then on the set, to sense what he or she will finally need from the actor. The subtle decisions of timing will then be made in the editing room. In Hollywood, films — especially comedies — are screened in front of trial audiences many times to get a measure of the precise timing that various moments need. We will discuss performance for the camera in the next chapter.

ACTING VS PERFORMING
For the first few years it is all an actor can do to make the script plausible, to make it come to life, to bring truth to the moments between herself and the other actors. It is only after many years, when all this has become part and parcel of her craft, that she can direct her attention to the effect she is having on the audience. That is a big moment in her development. It is something to be aimed for. It is the change from being an actor to becoming a performer. The first is purely involved with what happens on the stage, the second includes a concern with the perceptions, feelings and well-being of the audience.

Much of this chapter addresses the performer, but if you are a beginner it will not hurt you to be exposed to these ideas as well. So long as you understand that it may be a while before you can implement them.

The Audience Now Teaches Us

They are the final ingredient we needed to fashion our production. We will feel them watching, hear their reactions, sense their responses and see the play through their brains. We will discover new meanings, find more appropriate actions. We will realise that we must clarify this point, not overstate this moment. We will rediscover links between distant points in the play that we had forgotten about, or never even realised. The audience will tell us.

They do not know why they laugh and why they don't. They just do, and they don't. No individual member need have a clue about showbusiness. Yet en masse an audience is the most accurate measuring instrument of timing ever invented. It can smell a lie a mile away. All the performer needs to do is listen.

Early in a season I have at times heard an actor muttering 'The audience doesn't seem to like this show.' As though this were an immutable law of nature, a fact of life: here is the show, there is the audience, and they don't like it. To me this is a little bit like a tailor looking at a suit that he has just made, scratching his head and saying, 'This suit doesn't seem to fit my client.'

It is up to the tailor to make it fit. He has the material, he has the measuring tape. We have the play, we have the audience responses.

Building a Machine

The point of a scene between two good actors is not to interact well, plausibly, believably. That is a given, not an issue. Their aim in doing the scene is to affect the audience in particular ways. To take them through the journey of the scene.

I do not like the idea of a play being regarded as a series of speeches, inexorably trotted out, to be judged by an immutable audience. The sculptor moulds clay, the composer structures sounds. The actor is there to move the audience, carefully, precisely, consistently.

So long as we regard acting as delivering speeches interestingly, we will be on the back foot, wondering what they will think about the play. The moment we think of acting as presenting a series of moments of behaviour, everything changes. Remember that every moment of behaviour that you play on stage is a piece of information being sent to the audience. Suddenly it is no longer a question of what they will think. It has become our job to tell them what to think. We are the ones presenting the

MEET THE AUDIENCE

information to them. Not the other way round. In the first few weeks of playing we learn to:

1. Feed the right moment,
2. Wait the correct time, and
3. Feed the next moment

at every point of the play. With practice we will discover what the right moments are and the correct times. They will be the ones which allow the audience to feel that they have discovered the jokes for themselves, and the sensitive moments.

During the first few weeks of playing we are in fact *building a machine with which to emotionally move the audience through the journey of the play*. It is also a sculpture in time. If I sound callous, calculating and heartless forgive me. I swear that it takes a great deal of care, dedication and love to achieve.

THE GENERAL RULES REVISITED

In Chapters 9 and 10 I suggested rules of thumb for trying to realise a script. Here is an up-date.

- If we establish the central problem of the play clearly;
- If we set up a need in the audience for a resolution;
- If we provide adequate decoys to continually surprise the audience — in other words at each moment, we point the audience's attention in the direction the play seems to be going, rather than where it is going;
- If there is at least one character they can hang their hat on, that they can be interested in;
- If there is conflict — either goodies and baddies, or the Yin and Yang within one character;
- If the audience is held moment by moment;
- If there is always a need for the next moment;
- If everything builds to the final climax and resolution;
- If the final reverberation rounds off much of what has been touched on, if it resolves the themes;

then the show will work. It is as easy as that!

LET THE AUDIENCE IN

There are no more effective ways of engaging a child in play than by letting *her* affect *you*. If she says 'boo' jump, or faint, and you will have instantly made an interested and giggling friend. Because you allowed her to affect you; you endowed her with power. This is perhaps the strongest hook for audiences as well. To let them feel present, necessary, relevant.

It is a difficult transition to go from trotting out the predetermined ritual developed at rehearsals to a performance related to an audience. This is most obvious in a one-person show. There you can immediately see when the performer is charging on, locked into his routine, his set delivery, here a look, there a walk, everywhere a quack-quack! By contrast, it is so powerful when he has the courage to expose himself and allow the audience into his thoughts. But the same principles apply in a shared scene. There is no point in doing the next moment if the audience is not ready for it. Wait until they have received the present one. As your character you have a train of thought. We have to make sure this train of thought is also being followed by the audience. We must let them in.

When your character is in full flight of anger and you can't stop to make sure that they are with you, that simply means that the moment of allowing them in is after a tirade rather than after a single thought. That's alright. They will follow you. Your momentum will carry them. But as you catch your breath let them join you again. Never go too long without letting them in.

When your character is in a quandary don't immediately go on. Don't solve it for them by telling them what happens next. Allow the audience a moment to share in the problem. The instant you know that they have been exposed to the uncertainty, that they have been allowed to try to deal with it, you can go on. Now they are part of it too. It is momentary stuff, but crucial.

It is another little way of letting the audience see the show through your character's eyes.

WAIT FOR THE LAUGH

Waiting for a laugh is the most obvious way of letting the audience in. It is a question of finding a legitimate thought, a legitimate range of considerations to enable you to postpone the next line. This pause will of course seem to have nothing to do with the audience's presence. It will often be an extension of the follow through of the action that got the laugh, or the stunned response to the switch. But in fact the pause acknowledges them. It makes them feel welcome.

AUDIENCE GRAVITY

Whether deliberately or unconsciously, during the first few weeks of playing, the performance will alter because of the audiences' responses. Not all of our adaptations are constructive. Some are disastrous. By the third week of playing a show can be down to something like a third of the laughs it was getting on opening night. *Part and parcel of becoming accustomed to the audience is the overwhelming temptation to prepare for responses which they have not yet made.* It is a form of anticipation, more powerful than any we have yet met, coming as it does, not from simple habit, but from intimidation.

In order for the audience to laugh we have to break logical contact with them. During the hiatus we have to be prepared to disappear from their logical horizon for a moment, to leave them floundering. We have to trust that they will rejoin us once they have understood the joke and are laughing. That is frightening. They may have rejoined us last night. But what if they don't tonight?

We have all seen a self-conscious person telling a joke at a party. By the time he got to the punch line he was giggling so much the joke was totally incomprehensible. This is a person who is afraid to momentarily part company with us while he delivers the punch line. He would like to stay in touch with us. In fact he would like to join us where we would have been *if he had told the joke properly.* That is, laughing *with* us. The only problem is, we're not laughing because he didn't tell it properly.

Audience Gravity is the name that I give to this pull from the audience. They are like a dark ocean, silently pulling us towards their state of rest as we approach a laugh. We don't want to lose our link with them.

As we near the laugh that moment of discontinuity and vulnerability looms. It heads towards us like a brick wall, a sound barrier, we are going have to crash through. If we try to protect ourselves in any way at all, by ducking, slowing down, or swerving even slightly, we will kill the laugh.

The only way the joke will work is by us having the insane courage to drive through the critical moment at the excruciatingly correct pace, playing the correct action.

The correct pace and the correct action are those which arose naturally out of the situation. It is what we were doing at rehearsals before we knew there was going to be a laugh there at all.

To help describe what tends to happen as we unconsciously brace ourselves against a laugh let us look at David Williamson's play *Travelling North.* Frank and Frances are an elderly couple who, having left family and friends behind in the big city, have just arrived at their new home in a little fishing village on the north coast, to start a new life together. Frank does not suffer fools gladly. In scene 7 they are unpacking and singing the praises of their new haven.

FRANCES: I've never heard so many bellbirds.
FRANK: Yes, it's a regular little paradise. The edge of the lake is thick with black swans and ibis.
FRANCES: It's very, very beautiful.
FRANK: And the best part about it all is that there isn't another house in sight.
FREDDY: [*off*] Anyone at home?
   [FRANK *goes to the door*. FREDDY, *a jovial man in his sixties enters, wearing a bright shirt and shorts.*]
   G'day there. Am I intruding?
FRANK: No. I, er, don't believe we've met?
FREDDY: Freddy Wicks, your neighbour. I saw you'd arrived so I came across to see if I could lend a hand.
FRANK: That's very kind of you. I'm Frank and this is Frances.
FRANCES: I didn't realise we had a neighbour, Mr Wicks.
FREDDY: Freddy, please. No, you can't see me from here. I'm up the back there into the trees, so cheer up, you're not on your own after all.
FRANK: [*dully*] What a surprise.
FRANCES: Are you there by yourself?
FREDDY: Yeah. A happy marriage. A blameless life. Snuffed out like a candle. Makes you wonder.
FRANCES: Have you any children?
FREDDY: Yep. Two boys and a girl. They've all done well: one's a teacher, one's a lawyer and m'daughter married a Qantas pilot, but it gets a bit lonely up there all by m'self. But let's not be morbid. Would you like an ale?
   [*He deposits two beer bottles on a table.*]
FRANK: Well, perhaps a bit later. We're trying to clean this rubbish out.
FREDDY: I've got a ute up there. I'll bring it down and help you cart the stuff to the tip. I don't want to sound like a snob, but it's a great relief to have an educated couple like yourselves in here. I'm not saying anything against old Sam, God rest his soul, but he wasn't the sort of neighbour you could have an informed discussion with.
FRANK: He died here, I take it.
FREDDY: Yes, right there where you're standing. I was the one who found him. The poor bugger drank himself to death. The climate here's fine, but I find that if you don't keep your mind active you can get a bit morbid. Where do you two come from?
FRANK: Melbourne.
FREDDY: I had a cousin from Melbourne. Poor fellow shot himself.
FRANK: It can have that effect on you.
FREDDY: How long have you two been together?

FRANK: If you mean under the same roof, about an hour and a half.
FREDDY: Have you just married?
FRANK: No. We're living in sin.
FREDDY: Go on.
FRANK: You've got a ute, you say?
FREDDY: Yes, I could back in up the drive.
FRANK: That's very kind of you. The sooner we shift this junk out the better.

There are many wonderful moments in this scene but I will focus only on the following two.

FREDDY: Freddy, please. No, you can't see me from here. I'm up the back there into the trees, *so cheer up, you're not on your own after all.*

and

FRANK: He died here, I take it.
FREDDY: *Yes, right there where you're standing.*

We know how proud Frank feels at having bought a lovely old house, so isolated, so secluded, so snugly tucked away in the tress. When Freddy announces himself from off-stage Frank's heart sinks. By the time Freddy says, 'so cheer up, you're not on your own after all' that has become a very funny line.

There is also something extremely uncomfortable about being told that you are standing exactly where someone died.

COMMON MISTAKES ARISING FROM AUDIENCE GRAVITY

In the discussion that follows I am not referring to any actual performance that I have ever seen. I have tried to collate observations that I have made from many plays and productions, and to apply them to these two moments, to demonstrate the most common distortions we actors make as a result of Audience Gravity.

PULL BACK FROM THE LAUGH

'So cheer up, you're not on your own after all' works best as a welcoming line. Freddy is innocently cheering them up, offering his presence and his services. Neither of which, of course, Frank and Frances want. This is a moment when Freddy should look silly with no idea why. In 'pulling back from the laugh' the actor playing Freddy will instinctively tend to reduce his commitment to the situation. He will pull back from healthy actions like to welcome, to reassure, to celebrate, to bond, which would all work. He now softens it by playing something like: to make light of, to add as an afterthought, to share an irony, or worse, to apologise!

Not Follow Through

Freddy's follow through (see page 39) might be to beam at Frank and Frances reassuringly (I'm here at your service, you can depend on me). But as the actor becomes intimidated by the moment he might start to look away a little bit earlier, before he had even finished the line, thus again making his message less important, less committed.

This is one characteristic which the comedy legends have in common. Mae West, Buster Keaton, Chaplin, Lucille Ball, Jack Benny: they all followed through. It is during the follow through that they drove home to us the irrationality of the moment, and it is during the follow through that they allowed us the time to savour it.

Warn Them it's Coming

A way of pleading for the audience to laugh is to warn them the joke is coming. (But as with love, the more desperately you try to cling to it the more certainly it will vanish!)

Here Freddy might say, 'So cheer up!', leave a gleeful, anticipatory pause before 'you're not on your own after all.' (Boom boom.) The pause says to the audience 'Wait for this. I am about to say something wonderful.' The punch line will then land on hushed silence.

Central to this joke is the disparity between Freddy's genuine, intended goodwill and its actual effect on Frank and Frances. 'So cheer up' is important to set Freddy up as trying to welcome them. If his action becomes 'to announce', it will distort his character, and the credibility of the situation will be lost.

Warning an audience is rarely a good idea. They brace themselves and it is then very difficult to surprise them.

Spell it Out

We try to 'explain' the joke ever so slightly. So instead of the actor playing to cheer them up with 'you're not on your own after all' he plays 'to intrude on them', 'to impose his presence on'. That is indeed what the audience must see happen but it is *never* what Freddy must play. Williamson has written a wonderful ingenuousness into Freddy. He thinks he's helping. Playing an action like to intrude when he should be welcoming is also called doing the audience's job for them.

The audience should be allowed to discover the joke for themselves. If the actor tries to spoon-feed it to them they will turn their heads away.

Telegraph the Tag

The actor playing Frank might become a little anxious about the approaching laugh on 'Yes, right there where you're standing'. So when he said his own preceding line 'He died here, I take it.' he might inadvertently look down at his feet. That would kill the laugh.

'He died here, I take it.' means around this house generally. Freddy then uses 'here' literally: 'right there where you're standing.' If Frank had already looked down at his feet it would have subtly directed the audience's attention in the general area of the switch. This would severely reduce the surprise for them.

In relation to small children performing tasks, the great educator, Maria Montessori, said 'Any assistance that you give a child, that the child does not need, is a hindrance.' I think the same applies to audiences.

Repeat the Formula

Here we are again trying to repeat the form. In the desperate attempt to get the laugh again tonight, we try to pull the same face, give the same intonation as we did last night. Once the outward form becomes more important to the player than what it originally meant, the audience will see an actor trying to get a laugh. What they originally laughed at was a character in a predicament coping in a bizarre, inappropriate way.

> ## NEVER GO TO THE THEATRE ON A SECOND NIGHT
> Second nights are notoriously bad events for performers. The only reason we do second nights is to get to the third night. After the hype of Opening Night we now want to repeat last night's performance. But with the best will in the world, there is less adrenalin, and less at stake. So we sit and wait for the audience to respond as they did last night. But they don't because we are not doing anything to cause them to respond. We are waiting for *them*. Second nights are a chronic example of relying on the form. Of going directly for the end result.

Share the Joke

If the actor playing Freddy plays the action to share the joke with Frank and Frances, and laughs when he says, 'so cheer up, you're not on your own after all.' you can be pretty sure the audience won't laugh. Because he will have destroyed the tension of misunderstanding. He would again be deliberately intruding instead of helping out.

On the other hand if he laughs because he is *happy to be of service*, it can work. It is dangerous but it can work. Indeed, it can be terribly powerful because it makes him doubly stupid.

BREAKING THE TENSION

At the very heart of all the above problems lies this one basic principle: maintaining tension until the laugh occurs.

When a comedy moment depends on a line being thrown from one character to another it is very much a team effort. Because it depends not only on the delivery of the line, but also on the way it is received. When two people are involved there is no such thing as a funny line. There are only lines which have funny effects on other people. If the line doesn't impinge, it won't be funny.

Quite generally, near a comedy moment you can regard the theatre as a huge balloon. At that instant we need to momentarily increase the tension in the room. We need to increase the pressure in the balloon. Everyone involved in the action helps build that pressure. If any one person responds inappropriately that will act as a leak; the tension oozes out through that distraction and the critical pressure may never be reached.

A shrug, a giggle, a look away before the punch line or during the hiatus can all dissipate the tension. It takes courage to create a tension that you know they will burst in a moment with their laughter. It takes courage to play the moment with faith and commitment. In the follow through it takes courage to prove to them that this moment is not only important, but in so being, is also funny. It is, from the actor's point of view, a battle of wills. A battle which, I might add, the audience is only too happy to lose.

LEGITIMATE STRESS

A comedy moment generally does need to be made clear to the audience. All the above detrimental examples of highlighting the joke were wrong because they went against the truth of the moment. They reduced its authenticity. The truthful playing of it is what will guide you to the required stress of a word, or the appropriate turn of the head, or the moment of trying to regain orientation. A short-hand way of saying it is that we have to make absolutely sure that:

the stress on the punch line seems to comes out of the needs of the situation, never out of the needs of the joke.

Finally, good timing is playing the right *action* at the right time.

> ### SUMMARY FOR DEALING WITH AUDIENCE GRAVITY
> Audience Gravity looms like a wall of intimidation as you approach a laugh. The solution is:
> - To be very clear about what it was that made the moment funny.
> - To be adequately warmed up, alert and centred enough to be able to resist the pull of Audience Gravity and be able to play the appropriate actions, faithful to the situation.
> - To have the insane courage to drive through the critical moment at the excruciatingly correct pace.

CULTURE AND BOREDOM

Culture at the highest level may deal with subtle beauty, sophisticated notions, new modes of communication. As J. Z. Young (pages 1, 26) says 'Whoever creates new artistic conventions has found methods of interchange between people about matters that were incommunicable before'. Classical music and Shakespeare do require familiarity before they can be appreciated. Great art often makes a demand on an audience.

But here I want to make a confession. Most theatrical performances which will mystify you will not do so because they are presenting lofty thoughts. Rather it will be because we the actors and directors have not adequately done our homework.

What happens is that a writer like David Mamet will write dialogue which is an uncannily accurate representation of life. But at first reading it sounds difficult, non-sequiturial. Rather than investigate what it means, how those thoughts are connected, the actors will learn the words and utter them with confidence, and with intriguing cadences to make them sound 'interesting'. The audience will then sit there baffled by this incomprehensible gibberish. The actors are playing a game with the audience called 'I am allowed to baffle you and be obscure because I am doing art, and you have to sit there and take it because art is not always comprehensible.'

Dear audience, next time you feel intimidated by a piece of theatre, relax. There is nothing wrong with your abilities of comprehension. It is we on stage who have probably been expedient, and are now being pretentious to cover our mistakes.

BAD AUDIENCES

People do not generally pay good money to go to the theatre in order to hate a show. They go prepared to enjoy it and to respond naturally. There are exceptions such as Opening Night, when the audience is made up of people who see around four plays a week, who are there out of duty and because of professional and social reasons. Their responses cannot be expected to be the same as those of a general audience.

I have found that what we call a bad audience is often nothing more than people who do not understand how to take the show, people who may be intimidated by it, confused. The answer is not to get angry with them, nor to treat them with disdain. I have been in many shows where the actors just speed up their delivery in order to get to the pub a little sooner because there's 'bugger all happening up here on stage'.

The aim of the actor is not to turn a timid audience into a raucous one. It is to give every audience, whatever its make up, the full benefit of the journey of the play. It is to allow this particular group of people to enjoy and respond to the spectacle according to their capacity and desire. The audience may be made up of elderly people at a matinee, who will not respond as quickly, or it may be largely made up of school children, who won't buy the theatricality and need more direct, street-wise interactions. Whoever they are, a better solution than washing one's hands of them might be to listen to their needs, understand their hesitancy, and to gently take them by the hand and lead them into the story. A timid audience will rarely become raucous, but treated with patience, respect and goodwill I have seen very few 'bad audiences' not eventually blossom.

DON'T STAR — SERVE

Many years ago I found it difficult to maintain my commitment to a show once everything was going well! Until I felt I had them I would work my heart out. Once the audience was in tune with my character and was laughing at his funny moments my resolve would waver, I would lose impetus. More recently a similar thing befell me when I started performing in the one-man shows, *Double Bass* and

Sky. I would come out onto the stage wondering what on earth I had to do to justify all these people coming out in the evening to see this show. To come and see me.

The two cases are similar. In the first, my aim was to win the audience over, to gain their confidence, to prove to them that I was funny. Once I had achieved that I had nowhere to go. In the second, my aim was to fill the theatre, to be a star. (I won't overstate it — they were not large theatres.) Once the audience was there what had I to do? I was frozen.

The answer in both cases is: to serve the audience. That is the job of the actor. Not to win the audience's approval or admiration, nor to show them how funny you are, because once achieved these give you nowhere to go. The aim of the performer is not to take anything *from* the audience. It is to give. It is to give them this story, this life, this fairyland. All of it. The actor's job is incomplete until the audience's minds are in the precise mode that they are meant to be in, in the final instant of the show.

To gain acceptance is a dead-end. To star is paralysing. To serve is realistic. And most pleasant.

12
FILM & TELEVISION

While living in London I heard this true story of an English family on holiday in Paris. They felt that their six-year-old little boy was spending too much time in the apartment of the French family across the hall, watching their television. At one point when he wanted to go in yet again they forbade it. He said, 'But I want to go and watch television.' They said, 'But darling it's all in French.' He thought for a moment and said, 'But the pictures are in English.'

It is probably not too much to say that no human activity, no human invention, has been so effective in exporting a country's culture as cinema, and now television. It is certainly the reason that I became an actor. Long before I knew that theatre had a relevance to the whole community I was taken to films. I remember Johnny Weissmuller as Tarzan when I was very young and in my teens such actors as Marlon Brando, Danny Kaye, Anthony Quinn. These were the people I was emulating in the school plays.

The cinema, as the pinnacle of American showbusiness, was also a tangible expression of the American dream. Like boxing, this was one area in which 'anyone could make it'. The rags to riches story was affirmed by people like Charles Chaplin, Louis Armstrong and Marilyn Monroe.

To 'legitimate' actors of the theatre there has always been a love-hate relationship with Hollywood, as they watched people with pretty faces and indifferent talent gain astronomical success. Hollywood is simultaneously looked down upon and yearned for. Walter Matthau is quoted as saying, 'All you need to make it in movies is 40 good breaks.'

In the film *The Last Detail*, Jack Nicholson and his two companions are in a bar before it has opened for trading. The barman refuses to serve them so Jack Nicholson sticks a pistol under his nose to persuade him. Once the gun appears of course he does serve them. In the scene immediately following, as Nicholson and his two co-stars are walking down the street, Nicholson tries to justify himself. He tries to make light of the incident by bragging. He is giggling in a guilty, hysterical, adolescent way, as he tries to gain the approval of his two companions. He is saying things like, 'Did you see the look on his face when I pulled the gun?' When I first saw this moment I knew that I had never before seen anyone attempt to show a piece of behaviour on camera so raw, so open, so wild. And I couldn't imagine the ambience on the set immediately before the scene was shot in order to allow this to flourish.

Although I am best known in my own country from television I have actually spent most of my working life in the theatre in front of an audience. I have appeared in numerous Australian films, but with the possible exception of *Travelling North*, have no experience of working on quality, international films. I have no conception, for example, of the atmosphere on set, or the procedures involved in making films like *Kramer vs Kramer*, *Braveheart*, or even *La Haine*.

Nevertheless, assuming that the actor's internal processes are fairly standard, for what they are worth, here are a few observations.

THE CENTRE OF GRAVITY

The most fundamental difference between film and stage is that on stage you have to pump your energy out to the audience, whereas on camera you allow the audience to come to you. On stage the centre of gravity is in the auditorium. On film it is on the set, on the screen.

It is very difficult for a cinema audience not to notice a face three metres wide. To convey on film what is happening inside you, you need only *think* it and the camera will pick it up. This means that you need the precision, and the nimbleness to be honest. On stage you must first make sure that you have the audience's attention. It takes raw energy and concentration to engage them. Only then may you be able to 'just think it'. (Incidentally, I do believe that if you are on stage, silently crying, even a person at the back of a two-thousand seat auditorium is likely to look at you and feel disturbed, to feel somehow moved without perhaps even knowing exactly why.)

Another huge difference between theatre and cinema of course is that in theatre, on the night, you only ever get to do 'take one'.

KNOW THE WHOLE CHESS GAME

The economics of film requires that all scenes in a particular location be shot at around the same time. This makes sense. Rather than trundling the whole circus of crew, equipment, props, caravans and catering, back and forth from one location to another as the story unfolds in the script, the director goes through and marks all the scenes that occur in one location. Weather permitting these will then all be shot together. Once these are done the circus will move on to another location.

What this means to the actor is that the film is shot out of sequence. You will be grief stricken at the funeral long before you film the scene where your brother died. There is a skill required here. You don't know what the sequence of shooting will be until very close to the time. And it is always likely that there will be last minute changes, because the day that you were supposed to shoot the sunny beach scene it may very well be snowing.

To allow for this, it is a good idea to carry the whole chess game in your head, because at the last moment you may indeed be asked to shoot scene 32 instead of 17 as scheduled. You will then have to be very clear of exactly where in the overall picture it occurs — when was the last time the audience saw you? What has happened to you just before this scene? Therefore, what is your loading as you enter this scene — your preoccupation? What must your emotional state be by the end of the scene? If there is direct continuity between this scene and your preceding one, or your following one, then this knowledge is vital.

Let me give you a delicious example from the early days of Australian television. In a series called *Homicide* (around 1968) we used to film the exterior stuff some six weeks before video-taping the interiors in the studio. Often we had different directors for the two occasions. Because some young director had not checked up on what had already been shot outside (and the actor was obviously an idiot) we had the following sequence go to air. There is a violent fight inside a house. Our hero is beaten to a pulp. He slowly crawls across the floor away from his assailant towards the door, blood all over him, he drags himself up, turns the door knob, opens the door — we cut to the outside — he now leaps out of the house, runs down the garden path, jumps over the fence and disappears down the road! All because they had shot the outside escape before realising how beaten up he would be inside. (I have embellished it, but not by much.)

Without an overview it is also very easy to repeat a particular mannerism over and over just because 'it felt right on the day'. I appeared in a children's film in which the leading lady ended every scene by giving her screen husband a little peck on the cheek. Most of these pecks of course ended up on the cutting room floor, but even without them her lack of preparation made all her scenes look similar. By contrast see how strategically Dustin Hoffman's little anxiety squeaks are placed throughout the film *The Graduate*. They do not appear in every anxious scene.

Continuity from one scene to another and repetition of the same piece of business are the easiest things to deal with 'on the day'. What is not so easy to figure out is what exactly your character is doing there. What is he or she trying to achieve? As with our preparation for a stage play we must gain an overview of our character's journey through the film. Every scene has a function, an emotional shape. Together they add up to our performance. What is the scenic action which links this scene with your whole journey? What are the forces you are wrestling with; which emotions are you holding down; *what are the issues which your character is responding to here but which do not appear directly in this scene?* This is where your homework becomes glaringly obvious when you haven't done it. It only becomes apparent when the whole film is put together.

The Mental Path

In theatre, after performing for a few weeks the thought sequences you have to play become established. All you need to do is to bring them to life. By contrast the actor's performance on film or television is more like a glorified improvisation. You haven't actually rehearsed it and drilled it in. Nor has it been informed by audience response. It all happens 'on the day'.

It takes nimbleness and enormous courage to blunder around in an alien environment, in alien clothes speaking new dialogue, with very limited freedom of movement, and to make all of it look as though you live here.

While film is certainly improvisational, when it comes to a long speech it does not hurt to do your homework.

I played the father in a ten-part television drama series called *Palace of Dreams* for the ABC in 1984. We had a version of all the scripts before we started rehearsals and we taped over a period of 20 weeks — two weeks per episode. In the last episode my son died and my character had some wonderful, emotional stuff to do. Call it compulsive, but by the time we started rehearsals for the *first* episode I would have been able to tape those final weepy scenes of Episode 10. I did this homework because I wanted to understand the flow of my character through the whole series, to make sure that there was a shape, a journey. I also wanted to avoid wasting time 'on the day' figuring out *what* my character was doing, in order to be able to concentrate on just doing it honestly.

It is much easier to repeat a long emotional monologue if you have practised the sequence of emotional states that will have to be reached throughout the speech. References and emotions then almost go hand in hand with the words, the words do become almost incidental and the focus can indeed be on the fleeting thoughts necessary to trigger the behaviour. This form of preparation is much more time consuming than simply learning the words, but I know of no better way for me. It is like practising a slalom run. You familiarise yourself with each and every flag, each twist and turn so that you will have a fair chance of hitting every one of your mental and emotional marks at speed.

The joy is that however well prepared you are, on the day you will still have to survive on your wits. The luxury of novelty is always there. The surprise of the actual set, the director's input, the other person's actual responses. All these are the bonuses which alter and freshen your own perceptions.

But nothing can replace the maturation of a series of thoughts in a speech over time. I know of no other way of probing into the little nooks and crannies that your mind will stumble onto by simply toying with the sequence of thoughts in an unrushed leisurely manner. You can view the overall and savour the immediate and find ways of marrying the two in the most effective, efficient, natural way. This takes time.

CHARLES LAUGHTON

To me the quintessential example of cinema genius, which shows the marriage of elaborate preparation with blinding spontaneous creativity comes from Charles Laughton. There is a television documentary called *The Epic That Never Was*, on the making of the film *I Claudius* around 1937, which was never completed. In this documentary we can see Laughton's performance in one scene evolve from one take to the next. We see the extraordinary complexity of the pathway of his thoughts as he brings to life the stuttering, stumbling Roman emperor.

It is sad that this degree of accuracy and perfectionism in acting is counterproductive in the film industry. It would seem that Laughton's meticulousness and self-criticism in the end prevented the film from being completed. They saw that they were simply going to run out of time and money. I believe that a similar kind of problem befell another cinema genius towards the end of his career — Peter Sellers.

HITTING YOUR MARK

Once a scene is about to be shot you will have been rehearsing a particular set of moves, co-ordinating with the moves of a cameraman and a soundman holding the microphone on the end of a pole, called a boom. (I know modern technology has computerised limbs to move the cameras and microphones in the most extraordinary ways. I think the principles remain the same.) There is always a great to-do about whether the shadow of the microphone on the wall behind you is ever visible to the camera. Boom shadows are an absolute no-no. You are far more likely to do a second take because of a boom shadow than because of a bad performance. (I suppose the shadow is easier to judge.) Your movement during a take now has to fit precisely with what you and the camera and sound and lighting people have rehearsed. Your face has at all times to be in the right place, saying the right things if you are to be seen and heard. This is called 'hitting your mark'. For close-ups there is the extra restriction that any slight move in the wrong direction will put you out of focus. You will look blurry. In a two-shot (you and your fellow actor are both in the shot) a wrong move of the head may either have you disappear behind the other person or vice versa.

So, as you are shooting this quiet, intimate scene you are in fact surrounded by a crew of between 20 and 60 people. You are trying to handle your new adjustments, your new clothes and props while hitting your precise marks and holding your head where it has been decided. Through all of this, you must now find the soul of the story, you have to uncover the emotional truth of the moment and let it shine through in order to clearly and simply tell this little bit of the tale. That is film acting.

THE ACCIDENT

Film can capture an accident and give that to the audience at every screening. So often things go a little bit wrong but if you have the dexterity of mind and soul it is possible to turn the accident into something quite wonderful for the film. It has now become legend that in the playground scene in *On the Waterfront*, Eva Marie Saint accidentally dropped her glove. Brando picked it up, and in the course of the low-key flirting scene that ensues, he feigns handing it back to her. She doesn't know whether to take it or not. Every time she tries, he pulls it away. Because this teasing is so appropriate to their relationship in the scene, Elia Kazan, the director, printed that particular take and that is what we see in the film. It takes great confidence and imagination on the part of both actors to go with the accident and to capitalise on it. I have heard that in fact it was just Brando being a bastard and that Saint hated what she did in the scene. But it works beautifully.

WIPE AWAY THE LAST TAKE

When the director calls, 'Cut!' and then says, 'OK, that was good but I think we can do better. Let's go for another take straight away' — beware. If your character has gone through a big emotional change through the course of the scene, beware not to start the second take with the final emotion of the first.

Let us say that the scene is of you popping into your friend's house to pick him up to go fishing. The front door is open, which is not unusual, you go in, call out for him but no one answers. Let us say that this is all shot in one take. It is a little dark (mid-afternoon?) but there are no lights on. You wander through the house, come into the kitchen and find his mother lying dead on the floor in a pool of blood. Cut. Clearly your mood now is considerably different from what it was at the beginning of the take. The point is: make sure that you have wiped away the shock, grief and anxiety of the end of the scene before you come in for the next take.

This seems obvious but it is insidious. As the takes progress it creeps up on you. The final mood can leave more and more of a trace without you noticing, to the point where a person seeing only your seventh take would detect a wariness in you from the moment you stepped in the door. The Clarrie inside them would be yelling out, 'Why are you going in there? You obviously know that something spooky is going to happen!'

Be sure after each take to step away, to take a few deep breaths, relax. Go back into the holiday area of your brain. Reconstruct the innocence of simply picking your friend up. Busy yourself with incidentals like you hope he's ready — he's always late. 'We should have set out a bit earlier, there's not much light left.' 'I'm actually not all that keen on fishing — it gets boring. I only do this to humour him.' Anything to lighten the mood, to oppose anticipation, to deplete the opening moments of any undue weight or anxiety.

THIS SCENE DOES NOT LIVE ALONE

See if this rings a bell. A cowboy in a movie is walking across the yard on his way to do more chores. He makes a remark as he passes his friend who is standing by a gate. That remark leads to another which casually develops into a scene. But something looks slightly unnatural. When you think about it you realise the first cowboy came into the scene and settled himself with his elbows on the gate immediately after his very first casual comment. He knew back then that this was going to develop into a scene and he was making himself comfortable for its duration. Only the actor could have known that, never the character; he was going about his chores.

After many rehearsals of the one scene it is possible to lose a sense of its flow, in the scheme of things — of its momentum. You are seduced into playing this one scene as though it existed in isolation. Its moments become over-detailed, they become embellished, over-defined. They lose their dependency on what has gone before and they cease to set up what is coming after.

An incidental line like 'Excuse me, could you tell me the time?' can become an earnest attempt to enter into a meaningful conversation. Or it may become an over-tormented apology for the intrusion.

The answer is to remain very clear about where you have come from, where you are going and what the essential action is here. And then do your utmost to cling to the simplicity demanded by the natural flow of the story.

THE CORE OF THE SCENE

All scenes have one major point that the audience needs to learn. It is the reason for the scene's existence. With repetition it is easy to lose sight of this and to try find ways to make the scene 'more interesting'. My advice again is keep it simple. (Scenes often have more than one major point to make, but as with the spine of a play, it is very useful to distil a scene's function into one basic notion.)

Frank and Frances, to their chagrin, discover they have a neighbour (page 120). Danny tries to chat up Deborah — she makes it very difficult for him (page 75). This is what the audience must learn from this little section of the film. Be very clear what that information is. Make sure the crucial moment *is* clear and that the rest either lead up to it or flow from it. In the above scenes the two pivotal lines might be 'So cheer up, you're not on your own after all.' and 'Is someone taking up a lot of your time these days?'

DON'T CRY ON THE REHEARSAL

It is very tempting when you start out in the business to reassure yourself and everyone else of what a fine actor you are — at every possible opportunity. If, while rehearsing a scene for the camera in which you have to cry, you feel the tears coming, hold them back.

Don't audition during the rehearsal, and don't try to reassure yourself that you can do it, wait until the cameras are rolling. You may not be able to repeat it on the take.

From my experience, rehearsals on a film set are primarily for the camera, for the sound, for the lighting, not for the actors. Having done your homework you should only load up enough to show the crew what you will be doing. Give yourself just enough feeling to carry you through, to give everyone a good idea of the timing. *Do not do anything that you may not be able to repeat.* If you cry during the rehearsals only 17 people will see it. If you wait for the take, it will be witnessed by millions.

AFTER LUNCH SYNDROME

Filming on location can be gruelling: very early mornings, very long days and hard physical work. And yet, it can feel like summer-camp. Particularly after lunch, when people are pleasantly tired there can be a great sense of camaraderie. So when the first assistant says, 'Alright, back to work everybody.' there will be a few jokes and we will bestir ourselves. And when the director calls 'Action!' we will do the scene to the extent that it deserves given the pleasant atmosphere. After all, it is after lunch.

What we do not have is a programme note when the film is shown in the cinema saying, 'Ladies and Gentlemen, this bit was shot after lunch, so the actors were feeling very relaxed, that is why the scene drags a bit and is boring.'

It is important to realise that when they call action, when that camera rolls there are no excuses. That take may be what the audience will see. Make sure that it is what you want them to see.

THE EYES BEHIND THE LENS

It is tempting when on a film or television set to perform for those who are immediately at hand: the cast, the crew. Do what the director wants, give the other actors what they need, do what you can to make things easier for the crew, but do not insist on trying to entertain any of them. The entertainment is for the audience. These people on set have seen it evolve, they've seen it before. With the exception of the director they can no longer judge dispassionately. What I find useful is to think of thousands of eyes inside that little lens. Millions of people are packed in there and what they see is what must make them laugh and cry. It is a sense of their need, their reality which can help give you a solid sense of what you are doing amongst all this complicated, technological artificiality. I might add that it is to keep a sharp awareness of the audience that I regularly return to the stage.

BRING ON THE WORLD

To create the imaginary world for the audience inside the camera, I must first create it for myself. The only way I can get beyond the sense of the cables the camera cannot see, the premeditation of all of us actors, the intrusion of the crew, costumes, camera and props, is, before 'action', to create in my mind the imaginary world in which my character lives, and bring that onto the set with me. Some sense of who I am, what I want now as I come on, what I expect to find, what my mood is, what I have just done. Create this world and bring it on with you, and all the falseness around you will suddenly gain an underlying validity, a friendliness, a reason for being. It will suddenly all belong to the imaginary world because it is helping to create that world for the audience.

Creating your world helps you generate that first moment of truth on every take in film. It is equally vital to create it and bring it on stage with you in the theatre, especially in long runs.

13

LONG RUNS

Practice does not make perfect. Not always. We have seen that acting is made up of two skills: creating the character, and then maintaining it. It seems to be far easier to do the first than the second.

HABIT

I have mentioned playing the birthday boy, Harold, in *The Boys in the Band* very early in my career. We played it for *twenty-one months*. The cast was relatively inexperienced. Few of us had been in the business for more than three or four years. As the show ground on month after month, lapses of concentration brought about all sorts of quaint and bizarre errors. One night an actor making his entrance, appeared at the door with his hand near his waist, cupped in a strange position. He came in, was about to put my birthday present down, before he realised that his hand was empty. He'd forgotten the present in the dressing room. Yet he had stood at that door, waiting to come on stage, with his hand cupped appropriately as though holding the item. He said later that was why he didn't realise he didn't have it, because his hand was in the right shape!

At another point in the play an actor had to walk across the stage to make an exit. In Sydney the trip took him something like seven steps. When we transferred to Melbourne the stage was considerably narrower and the journey required only about four steps. At the first performance in Melbourne, sure enough, the actor took his normal seven steps! He was nearly walking on the spot to fit them all in. But without the thought of what the character was actually doing at that moment, the comfortable, habitual thing to do was to take his usual number of steps.

Nature has given us a very powerful tool to help us through life. After we have learned to walk we no longer have to think what our legs are doing when we want to go to the fridge. We do not need to think of the accelerator or the brake when we drive. Just the road.

RITUAL

Similarly society has spared us the trouble of having to re-invent frequently performed behaviour, or behaviour with momentous emotional loading. It allows us to ritualise difficult occasions like weddings and funerals ceremonially, and casual, everyday interactions with phrases like 'Hello.' 'How are you?' 'Very well, thank you.' 'See you tomorrow.' Imagine trying to exchange these simple social strokes without the convenience of these little ritual phrases!

Highly charged occasions such as birth, death and marriage are given structured form. Religious leaders would be hard pushed to come up with appropriate, original sentiments every time they had to officiate at such occasions. Therefore the religion devises an appropriate ritual to commemorate the event, which also gives the people going through the pain or joy a structured outlet for their emotions.

We use shorthand. Regular behaviour done frequently becomes habit; that which is too emotional we ritualise. It makes things easier.

In everything but acting.

When we have been playing a role for any length of time these two 'aids' to our everyday existence — habit and ritual — conspire to make life extremely difficult. The physical behaviour becomes habitual; the accompanying intentions, thoughts and emotions all but disappear, and we are dragged back into repeating the form; the move, the gesture, the intonation. Finally, the performance tends to be reduced to a ritual — a mere symbol of the life we started with. It is a dry, brittle, empty shell.

Two lines in T. S. Eliot's poem 'The Hollow Men' brilliantly evoke for me the essence of performances in a long run:

> Shape without form, shade without colour,
> Paralysed force, gesture without motion;

I think that the fundamental culprits are the following two thoughts:
- I must repeat what I did last night; and
- I must feel it again as freshly tonight as I ever have.

These two, seemingly logical demands, are guaranteed to destroy your performance.

WE COMPARE IT TO LAST NIGHT

Imagine that for some reason you had to hold your right arm out horizontally at one point in the show. One night your arm is slightly lower than it should be. It is not horizontal. The stage manager tells you that your arm was a little lower tonight, could you make sure that it is a little higher tomorrow night? So the following night you think of holding your arm a little higher than last night. You do the same the following night, and the night after that. The result is that as you keep thinking of holding your arm 'a little higher' you will find that before very long your arm is pointing to the ceiling.

The problem lies in guiding your performance tonight by comparing it with what you did last night. Rather than by thinking about it in the more objective terms of what it is that the audience needs to see.

WE TRY TO FEEL IT AS FRESHLY

When you first play a moment in rehearsals — let us say it is of anger — you are a little shocked. It is new, daring and exciting. You experience it strongly. It is not often that we are given licence to behave angrily in this society and the fact that it is new gives it resistance, it forces us to explore how far we should go with it, we are constantly pushing barriers as we arrive into untrodden emotional territory. This sense of daring is short lived. As soon as you have done it a few times and it is no longer new you would need to become a little angrier to achieve the same inner sensation. As you became used to that second level you would need to become angrier still to get the same feeling again. The point is that your system progressively becomes immune to each level of anger. As time goes on your inner sensations become utterly useless as a guide to your performance.

In the early seventies I saw a production of *Fortune and Men's Eyes*, which is set in a prison. The prime concern of the director and the actors was indeed that they should all 'truly feel it' at each and every performance. I caught it towards the end of its 10 week season by which time it had degenerated into incomprehensible bellowing. It did not so much depict the rage of frustrated criminals, disenfranchised by society, as the ineffectual antics of actors desperately trying to be even more 'real' than they had been the night before.

I think that William Shakespeare must have seen that production, because he has Hamlet say (Act III scene 2):

> O! there be players that I have seen play, and heard others praise, and that highly, not to speak of it profanely, that, neither having the accent of Christians nor the gait of Christian, pagan, nor man, have

so strutted and bellowed that I have thought some of nature's journey-men had made men and not made them well, they imitated humanity so abominably.

We do have to have the 'real' feelings. But that does not mean new feelings. Just the right feelings.

YOU CAN'T FEEL IT EVERY NIGHT

On the other hand there is a comforting myth in the industry that you can't feel it every night. I think that is wrong. You can. It's just very hard. But just as the singer can hit the note when required and the acrobat can do the full-twisting back somersault it is possible to revisualise a reference night after night. The *sensation* of the feeling may become diluted as you become acclimatised to it, but your tears will still be real, your laughter still genuine. Once a day you can think of the Eiffel Tower and see it momentarily. The reference only ceases to work if you allow your concentration to wander and allow the more repetitive things around you to intrude. (If a reference does dry up there are always hundreds of others that will do the job.) There is only one fundamental requirement here: concentration. To achieve a high state of concentration you need to prepare.

THE AUDIENCE IS A BLOB

After a very short time the presence of the audience in the auditorium can become almost incidental. They can easily become this big, black, disembodied blob which responds now and again, it would seem, almost arbitrarily. But we persist because the show must go on.

This no doubt is the crux of the whole problem. The moment we lose focus of the audience we can only continue by monitoring ourselves from inside, but that is like trying to steer a car by looking at the dashboard. You will crash. The audience is the road. It is the recipient of our performance and our only guide. Only they can keep you simple, natural, honest and real.

TAKE *THEM* THROUGH IT

Ignoring them makes the job of acting in a long run odious. It becomes a mindless ritual to be ground through night after night. The situation changes completely when we see the task as doing things *to* the audience. We go from thinking of the performance as putting *ourselves* through a series of antics, to taking the *audience* through the moments of the story.

We now replace the two demands:
- I must repeat what I did last night; and
- I must feel it again as freshly tonight as I ever have.

with three questions:
- How does the audience feel at this moment?
- What does this next moment in the play signify?
- How can I most simply and honestly realise that moment for this audience?

In this way we dislocate ourselves from our own internal, unreliable criteria and follow the much more relevant ones of the audience's needs and perceptions. This is never boring. Because the audience is real, dangerous and very hard to gauge.

To follow this approach we need:
- a window into the audience's hearts and minds at each instant; and
- a clear picture of the next moment of life that they need to see, in order to take them through this little bit of the journey.

For *the window into their hearts* there is an entity which I find useful called the 'Third Eye'.

THE THIRD EYE

Clarrie, that irreverent, anarchic teenager living inside you (Chapter 9), was a useful concept during rehearsals as a truth barometer, guiding you, whispering 'What you are doing is bullshit. It looks like acting, it sounds like a reading.' or 'That felt honest. That smelt like life.' If Clarrie were to sit in the audience now and sense *them* she could keep you in touch with their perception and their needs. You would have a firm basis for your momentary decisions, you would always know where you stood. This entity which sits out there and watches you, which ruthlessly senses the audience and then guides your next moment is what we call the Third Eye.

This is a very dangerous concept for beginners. It will be 10 years before a little part of you can sit out there in the audience and watch the rest of you here on stage, working.

My acting teacher told us a lovely story. A psychologist was alone in a room with a chimpanzee. There was a bunch of bananas in the corner, and the psychologist was typing at a typewriter. For three days he typed and the chimpanzee watched. Every now and again the chimp would go to the corner and grab a banana. On one such occasion, as the chimp's back was turned the psychologist quietly slipped out of the room. He wanted to see what the chimp would do with the typewriter. So he kneeled down to the keyhole and looked through. Do you know what he saw? A little brown hairy eye looking right back at him.

The moral is that if you try to watch your performance too early in your career all you will see is yourself watching yourself. But eventually the Third Eye will provide you with your ear into the audience's heart. In a long run it will become your oasis, your umbilical cord.

THE BEHAVIOUR CAPSULE

The theatre is a laboratory. There are few situations where human responses can be as carefully monitored and observed as in the theatre. The actor has the rare luxury, night after night, of being able to ever so subtly vary the playing of a predetermined set of moments. We have access to a controlled experiment: How will the audience respond if I play this moment like this instead of like that?

What becomes apparent is that at each moment there are certain clear limits of behaviour within which the cues we send to the audience will work, and outside those limits of behaviour the moment won't work. A moment can be a shrug, a sentence or a double-take. Whatever you consider to be a beat of life. As we test night after night we will discover, for example, how long we need to take to recover from a particular moment of surprise in order for the audience to believe it. And how short a time before they begin to doubt us. How angry do we have to become at another point? How laidback before the audience doesn't care either?

In the first few weeks of a run I regard it as our job to carry out this painstaking research, in order to establish a very clear notion of the envelope associated with each and every moment of the play. Behaviour within that boundary will convey to the audience what needs to be conveyed at that moment. Step outside it and you lose them, or confuse them. Your whole performance then takes the form of a string of beads, a series of moments of behaviour, little packages of life, each clearly defined by its allowable boundary. Each such moment I call a Behaviour Capsule.

Here is the power of this concept. Human beings are breathtakingly flexible in their behaviour. They can convey the same piece of information to one another in a virtually limitless number of ways. The inflection can vary ever so slightly but be compensated for by a tiny difference in the eye message or physical gesture. The possibilities seem infinite. This means that once we have a clear image of the envelope within which we can operate for each moment we have an almost infinite choice of exactly how we will play it. So long as we stay within the boundaries of the Behaviour Capsule we can actually *improvise*. We can take any path we wish within a very finely structured context. (Robert Schumann said of Johannes Brahms that he was able to achieve such tremendous freedom within such a strict discipline.)

That freedom is how the Behaviour Capsule becomes invaluable in helping us respond to information gleaned by the Third Eye. You have an awareness of how the last moment has just affected this audience. You know how you yourself feel at this moment. *You know where the audience needs to be by the time you have finished playing this coming moment.* Within the confines of the Behaviour Capsule you now have infinite freedom as to how you choose to play it.

You can see why I regard improvisation as such a powerful teaching tool. Because at the end of the day I regard all of acting as a series of minutely controlled improvised moments. Disciplined accidents, guided by the needs of the text, the state of the audience, what the other actor has just done and my own frame of mind right now.

This approach requires great concentration. You pay for this microscopic freedom by having to make a split-second decision before every single moment. Clearly, this requires alertness; mental and emotional agility. These can only be achieved by thoroughly warming up (next chapter).

Accidents

The approach lends itself very well to dealing with accidents and the unexpected. It is flexible because one is not thinking in terms of long paragraphs, but in tiny moments. In the play *Three Hotels* I was alone on stage, doing one of my monologues one night, when a very large cockroach joined me. The theatre only holds around 200 people so the audience is very close, and they are above and virtually all around you. Naturally, they were riveted by my co-performer. It was impossible for me to ignore him without losing the audience's faith in my reality. My character was feeling angry and defeated at that point anyway so at an appropriate moment I stamped on my co-star.

Though you don't think of the process so formally while you do it, what happens is that you find a capsule in which stamping on the cockroach would not be too inappropriate, and you just bend the boundaries of that capsule momentarily to accommodate that action. The end result should be the killing looks as though it were simply part and parcel of the life of your character.

I once saw a performance of Shakespeare's *Henry IV*, by a very good company, in which an actor was doing a soliloquy next to a wine cask, the tap of which had accidentally been left very slightly open. He stood there talking to us as a pool of red liquid was slowly spreading over the stage not two metres away from him. Given that he was playing a character presumably aware and alive, the gently dribbling wine called him a liar. It was not what he had rehearsed, so this very experienced actor was prohibited from doing anything about it. He was paralysed. He obviously found it impossible to incorporate the turning off of a wine tap with his important speech. Ignoring it made nonsense of his character's credibility. We all know that what he was saying to the audience was 'Please ignore the accident over there and just listen to my words.' Unfortunately they did neither.

Plant a Flag

When you have to deal with an irregularity in your performance, like waiting for someone to get to their seat when they have come in late in a small theatre, or stamping on a cockroach or turning off a tap, it is very easy to lose the thread of where you were before the distraction. Often I have accommodated the intrusion only to find that afterwards I was lost, had no idea of what I had been talking about. A solution is to plant a mental flag the instant before you deviate from the script, from the norm. Give yourself a moment to think of the very next beat that you must rejoin when the interruption is over, and plant a little red flag there. Simply making that effort will see you home safe and sound after most emergencies.

Preparation Each Evening

Having spoken of the concentration required, I know of nothing more difficult than to come into a theatre night after night and to rip one's brain open in order to see the play afresh for a new group of people; in order to be able to sense them and make correct split-second decisions. Ripping your brain open (as I call it), before the show, is the only way I know to consistently give anything like a spontaneous performance in a long run. By that I mean warming up: mentally and emotionally as well as physically and vocally. That is the hard part, and the only hard part, of acting. It is brutally difficult to remove the inertia before the show, and to scrape away the barnacles from the night before. But once warmed up acting is easy — and for me always exhilarating. It is what enables you to make friends for a couple of hours, with a room full of total strangers, by becoming children again, by sharing a story, by creating magic.

14
WARM UP

Whenever I teach, because I put such emphasis on the warm up, I am invariably asked how one does it. I cannot in honesty end this book without addressing this vital subject.

There must be thousands of different ways of warming up, depending on your temperament, background and needs. My main reason for warming up, quite frankly, is that I am a coward. I lack confidence. I am terrified of becoming self-conscious, of thinking slowly, of forgetting my lines, of freezing up. More important, of losing the audience and boring them. If I am not sufficiently warmed up I tend to trip over words and fumble them. On the other hand, my early experiences of performing were often linked with acrobatics. That demands a very strict and disciplined preparation if you are to be able to think fast enough, and also if you are to avoid ripping muscles and tendons. This may have created a pattern for me. Learning transcendental meditation some years ago I think has also left traces which I employ.

I don't know what people do before they appear, ashen faced, at the top of the slalom run at the Winter Olympics, or before they walk out onto Wimbledon Centre Court. But they do something because their faces don't look normal. They look grim, focussed, alert.

On the film *Travelling North* I saw Leo McKern just before a take, close his eyes, give his head a sharp little shake and puff out a little burst of air, and he was ready to go. I was intrigued because this is a simplified version of something I do.

I was similarly surprised by a Tai Kwan Do instructor, who in warming up to do a demonstration, slowly hissed air out through closed teeth. This again is similar to one of the procedures I use. I can only assume that there are really not that many different ways for the human psyche to warm up. Totally independent approaches really do lead to surprisingly similar solutions.

Because the mental aspect of the warm up is so shrouded in mystery I am prepared to make a complete fool of myself here by trying to describe the antics I go through to try to get myself ready. I have no idea of what exactly these activities do; I can only say that they are the result of many years of trial and error, and that for me they work.

WHAT IS THE AIM OF THE WARM UP?

1. To focus your mind so that it can precisely conceive what it needs to conceive.

2. To centre yourself; to create a strong indestructible central core which will be able to withstand any distraction, any pressure without losing focus.

3. To mobilise the voice, the body, the brain and the emotions so that they are able to do whatever you call upon them to do. The whole system must be galvanised.

4. To have the fore-brain ripped open to be totally sensitive to the audience. To be open to the sense of their presence, thoughts and needs, as well as to those of your fellow actors.

5. To have the courage to be able to crash headlong into the brick-wall of the future. To act whole-heartedly, while blinded to the next split second.

RESULTS OF THE WARM UP

To Arouse the Emotions

When a dancer is warmed up they have the capacity to do the splits. They may not need to do them in the ballet but they are warmed up so that they could. Apart from his voice and body the actor warms up in order to have every emotional state at his finger tips before going on stage. All feelings are lying there just under the surface, waiting to be triggered.

To Alert the Mind

A three times world billiard champion said in an interview that 'billiards is a question of playing a series of easy shots. If that's not what you're doing then you're not playing billiards.'

You psyche yourself up to be able to think fast slowly, as happens while you are falling off a bicycle, and the whole event goes into slow motion; to put yourself into a state of mind where you have a long time to experience lightning moments. It is the fight-or-flee state.

Build an Inner Pressure

When you go out in front of a theatre full of people you feel a tremendous pressure coming from them — their presence, their judgment, their scrutiny.

When you warm up you build up a pressure inside yourself to balance the pressure from the audience. When the internal and external pressures are equal you can go out on stage and appear to be functioning normally.

Life and Death Motivation (for Everyday Behaviour)

Watch people talking and observe the casual, total impulse associated with each new little thought. It comes as a sharp edge of behaviour even when there is nothing important happening. In real life we can be casually and totally focussed on what we are doing. There is no competition from elsewhere for our attention. We simply do things.

When acting we are not only repeating premeditated behaviour but we are also operating within a multitude of constraints; there are thousands of things to distract us and millions of reasons to be self-conscious. It is to overcome these powerful intrusions and to regain the simple and total focus on what we are doing that we need razor sharp concentration. In fact, we need life and death motivation — simply to make our behaviour look actual, spontaneous and easy.

For what it's worth, here's what I do.

WARM UP

1. *Warbling*: In the car on the way to work I go through the various singing and speech exercises to get the voice warmed up and the tongue and the lips ready for action.

2. *Shoulders and Neck*: There are any number of ways of loosening up with gentle head rotation exercises, shoulder rolls and arm rotations. A favourite of mine is rotating the arms in opposite directions. Start with both arms straight up, let the right arm go forward and the left arm go backwards. They will reach the bottom at the same time. Keep them going till they meet again at the top. This is wonderful for the shoulders as well as for coordination. After ten one way do the next ten the other way (i.e. right arm backwards and left arm forwards). It is not a flurry of arms exercise; it works best as a gentle, deliberate, disciplined rotation.

3. *Pacing*: Now I start the long walk — the prowl. While doing it one day a phrase came into my head: 'Like a lion, in a cage, in a rage, on stage.' A bit cute perhaps but that is what one is heading for. Total focus, total fluidity, total power, endless possibilities. For

me, pacing is the major part of the warm up. Everything else is peripheral to this long, focussed journey to preparedness.

4. *Wrists*: As you pace you can gently shake your hands as though shaking water from them. I thought that keeping the wrists warm while pacing was just a little idiosyncrasy of mine, a carry-over from my tumbling days. As an acrobat doing rows of flip-flaps (back onto the hands, onto the feet) the most vulnerable areas that must be kept warm are the wrists. But I have come across this interesting piece of information. The hands, mouth and feet are responsible for a large part of the information coming into the brain; in fact the largest part aside from vision and hearing. Think how sensitive your hands and feet are to touch, and your mouth and lips to touch and taste. That implies that there are huge numbers of nerve endings in these areas reporting back to the brain. Presumably warming up your hands, feet and mouth stimulates a major part of the brain cells involved in *receiving* information. Pacing, shaking your hands and blowing raspberries will make you alert — and it works!

5. *Expire*: Now we come to the weird stuff. One of the first progressions from the simple pacing and wrist shaking and shoulder rolling is to stop for a moment and gently force air out through the mouth from deep down in the body. You can blow it out or grunt it out. But it must be slow, deliberate; not a cough or an explosion. This has a gentle sort of centring effect on me.

6. *The shock*: In the middle of walking, as unpremeditatedly as possible, suddenly shake your shoulders. One short, sharp shake. The shudder will send little waves down your arms. Even your head will jerk slightly. Do this also at some point in the middle of expiring air as explained above. As you are letting it out, suddenly shake the shoulders. A little grunt of air will burst out and then the air flow will stop for a moment. I think what this does is to alert me to shock. It prepares me for surprise. It prepares me to surprise myself. This is when you begin to feel the warm knot in the pit of your stomach, as the blood leaves the internal organs and goes to the muscles, ready for action. Use 'the shock' sparingly and with respect.

7. *The silent scream*: This is an extension of the expiring. Stop pacing for a moment. You now growl the air out through clenched teeth, almost as if in pain. The fists may also be clenched, elbows in tight to the body. You will want to take a couple of grabs of this at a time. The second and third not as strong as the first. In terms of chest and mind this is similar to what we do on the roller coaster as

it reaches the top and is about to drop away from under us. We push downwards, shouting, so that our souls contribute to the descent rather than having the air sucked out from under us along with the roller coaster. Be careful not to damage the vocal chords as you do your silent growling and screaming. If you are somewhere where you can shout, well and good, let it out every now and again. You are now liberating the wild animal. I repeat, be careful not to get carried away. No point in being all psyched up but with no voice left and a pulled shoulder muscle.

    8. *The flight to infinity — and rip.* Now stop for a moment. Close your eyes. Roll them back a little if you can. Again not too far! Breathe gently. Imagine that from inside your skull your forehead is at infinity. In other words viewed from inside, your forehead is at the edge of the universe. Now think of a point in your brain, a point

of consciousness flying out towards that infinite boundary of your forehead. It will never reach it but it flies off further and further towards it. After a second or two you rip yourself out of the process (as in point 6 above). Again you do it with a shudder of your head and shoulders, and then you open your eyes. This is what I call 'ripping the brain open'. Be careful with this one. Don't make the shake too brutal after that gentle, mental soaring.

Where all the previous antics have focussed me inwards and revved up internal engines, I think that this one prepares me more for outward focus. It generates a pin-point of concentration to the outside world; it aims at extreme sensitivity to the surroundings; to be alert to the thousands of little cues being sent by the audience and the other actors. Cues that will finally guide and feed the performance. It will also sharpen the ability to concentrate on this little moment.

As I pace, and it may take anything from between 10 and 50 minutes, depending on how well I know the show, I will tend to do a mixture of all of the above as feels appropriate. The warm up is a mixture of facing the cold, harsh realities of what you are about to do and a positive pumping up of confidence.

FINAL THOUGHTS BEFORE GOING ON

As we come closer to the moment of truth I find the following notions useful.

1. MATCH THE CABBY

The patrons have no doubt left a babysitter at home, they have had dinner, they have just tipped the cab driver and they are now here. Their sense of human truth comes from these interactions. If you want them to believe you now as you step on stage: match the cab driver. Don't give them some fake behaviour and ask them to pretend it's real. However stylised the show reassure them with simple street honesty at the outset.

2. DO IT AGAIN

It is the nature of this job that having gone through the whole show last night or at the matinee a couple of hours ago you now have to go through it all over again. Having established a rapport with the previous audience you will now be faced by a stone cold new group with whom you have to start the romance all over again. That is theatre. These people have paid too; they deserve exactly the same care and love as you gave the last group.

3. Shed the Dead Skin — Scrape Away the Barnacles

Every few weeks the form of how we do things solidifies (our intonations, gestures). We tend to come on stage to play the form instead of the scene. The outward behaviour has become encrusted, a dead skin around the performance; barnacles, which must be removed. When this happens we must have the courage to:

- Rethink *what* we are doing (i.e. rediscover what actions we are playing, what information we are imparting to the audience at any moment), and
- Discard *how* we are doing it.

We must trust that the right thoughts *will* regenerate more or less the correct form. We must shed the dead skin, and dare to come on stage pink and soft and bare, focussed on the heart of the moment, and open to anything.

4. When You Don't Feel Like It

There are nights when you have a splitting headache, or are extremely tired or just don't feel like doing the show. Two thoughts help me.

- Any fool can do well when everything is fine. It is only when things are bad that you discover the true champion.
- If a fire broke out in the theatre right now you would suddenly be filled with enormous energy. You could leap over tables to get out. If you were dropped in the desert you would have sufficient resources inside you to keep you alive for a week without eating. You are full of energy. Use it!

5. Fear

There are sometimes moments of panic just before going on. What if I forget my lines? Or faint? Or have a heart attack? My answer to myself is:

It happens. People have had epileptic fits on stage, some have no doubt gone beserk and run around with an axe, and yes, some have even forgotten their lines. (In fact, you have yourself.) That is part of life. Accept it. If you die, you die. In the meantime, go out there and see if you can avoid it. Accept the danger. Make friends with it.

6. Don't be Perfect

As you aim for precision, don't whip yourself up to the point where you cannot walk on stage. It is possible to psyche yourself into such a state, that you can no longer move. You freeze up. If that happens pull back totally. Forget brilliant. Rediscover ordinary. Aim at just doing it. Far more important to get on stage and do an ordinary show than to stay off stage and remain brilliantly frozen. Besides, if your normal performance is good then just doing it ordinarily will still be good.

THE WILD ANIMAL

It is impossible to face and move 500 souls without this insane daring, which I call the wild animal inside you. It is vital to any exciting performance. It is what generates the electricity, the accident, the volcano. During the warm up what you are in effect doing is letting the animal out of its cage. Because you are going to need it on stage with you — its power, its daring.

But what do you do with it after the curtain comes down? After you walk out of the stage door what do you do with this wild animal still raging to go, wanting more raw meat, more centre stage, more attention, more excitement?

You lock it up.

The alcoholic wards and divorce courts have been very well frequented by ex-actors who, I would suggest, allowed themselves to be dominated by the wild animal. My point is that you don't need to ruin your life to be a good actor. You simply need the discipline to gently lead the beast back into its cage after the show, close the door, lock it and put the key in a safe place.

But for God's sake don't lose it. You will need it again tomorrow night.

---

7. THE OPEN WOUND

The end of the warm up is not a conclusion. It is an open wound, which will only be healed by the audience in the final moments of the play. The warm up leaves you feeling capable, ready, but slightly off-balance. If you feel that sense of forward impulse — it is an ache, an openness — don't close it. Let the audience do that for you through the journey of the play.

8. CREATE THE WORLD

Now, moments before going on, fill your mind with the world you will be taking on stage with you, and the first moment of your life in that world. Where has your character come from? What is he expecting will happen when he goes on stage? Load up your very first feeling of the scene (remember — load it up then fight against it). Prepare your first line, but only your first line; the first action you will play; the walk with which you will enter. (This first moment may well have been hovering in your head from the beginning of pacing. That's fine.) I suppose this is what people would call 'getting into character'. I resist calling it that because in this state you could virtually play anything you wanted to.

9. THE AUDIENCE
There are four phrases which crop up in my mind in the last instants before going on.
- These people (in the audience) are real.
- Talk to them.
- Tell them the story.
- Let them feel it's real.

10. CALM BEFORE THE STORM
Just before stepping onto the stage or set, take a deep breath and let everything go. The insides are all ready to fire; you are totally alert and galvanised for action. Now stop everything. Drop all tension. Relax and love the business.

A FINAL WORD I LEAVE WITH MY PUPILS

1. Observe the world. To keep in tune with your audience, to observe the games people play, to collect characters and sense memories.

2. Keep your heart in the gutter and let your soul reach for the clouds.

3. Audiences love life and death struggles — people stretched to the limit: gladiators and trapeze acts, Wimbledon tennis and perfectly sung arias. That is our job. The world can function with alright accountants, doctors and electricians. But it finds very little use for mediocre art.

4. Warm up. In order to take the audience to fairyland split second by split second one has to think very fast indeed. It is a two hour slalom run. For that, one has to be thoroughly warmed up.

5. Humans are fascinated by seeing another soul. Rip yourself open and you will show them all souls. Through your own life, your own pain, your own dreams.

6. By showing them a truth about the character you're playing, you will show them a truth about themselves that they may have forgotten or ignored or never really known.

7. Never be satisfied with depicting a piece of behaviour in a hand-me-down way, in a manner currently accepted. Try to find a way that is truthful to you. You won't succeed but your attempts will get closer and closer through the years.

8. If the writing is good and what you do is true, simple and specific to this audience you will captivate them all, regardless of their taste, background or degree of sophistication.

RAISE THE CURTAIN

APPENDIX
Some Names of Actions

To accept (idea or person)
To accommodate
To accuse
To acknowledge
To adlib
To admit
To advise
To ally
To announce
To anticipate (head them off)
To apologise
To assess
To assure
To astound
To back off
To back them up
To back track
To bear with
To blame
To brace oneself
To break the ice
To bring someone down to earth
To brush off
To bucket (tip garbage over)
To build them up
To cajole
To call a spade a spade
To call foul (protest)
To call to order
To case ('the joint')
To catch them out
To challenge
To change the subject
To chastise
To check (query)
Th chop off at the knees
To clarify (explain)
To clear one's name
To cling onto the initiative
To close in (on them)
To clutch at straws
To come clean (admit)
To commiserate

To comply
To concede
To conclude
To confess
To confide
To confirm
To confront (hold mirror up)
To confuse (issue or person)
To consider (weigh up)
To conspire
To convince
To corner (trap them)
To correct (the other person)
To cover up (emotions)
To crush
To cut the crap
To dangle the carrot (entice)
To defend
To define (an issue)
To defy
To deliver an ultimatum
To denounce
To derail
To direct
To discover
To discredit
To dismiss (the issue or them)
To disrobe
To draw out (the other person)
To drive the point home
To elaborate
To embrace
To enthuse
To entice
To evade
To father (look after)
To feel out
To fill them in (explain)
To flatter
To forbid
To force an answer
To force the issue
To gather one's forces

To get attention
To get back to business
To get down to business
To get one's bearings
To get out from under
To get them back on track
To get a toe in the door
To give an inch
To give evidence
To give them enough rope (to hang themselves)
To go along with
To grab their attention
To head them off (at the pass)
To highlight (a point)
To hold up as evidence
To home in (on them)
To humour them
To imply (meaning or thought)
To impress
To improvise
To include (the other person)
To insinuate
To insist
To justify
To keep them at arm's length
To keep them at bay
To keep them in check (chess)
To keep them on the hook
To kick oneself
To lay down the rules
To lay the cards on the table
To let them stew
To 'look ma, no hands'
To maintain control (self/other)
To make peace
To make them feel at home
To minimise
To mobilise the troops
To moralise
To mother (care for)
To muster the troops
To new tack (change course)
To nurse
To object
To offer
To offer a compromise
To offer a way out
To oppose
To organise

To override
To paint the picture
To pass the buck
To pay back in kind (tit for tat)
To pay lip service to
To persist (in playing an action)
To pinpoint
To pin them down
To placate (to calm)
To plead innocent
To prevent
To probe
To protect
To protest
To prove
To provide evidence
To pull the rug (from under them)
To pull them up (stop them)
To size up (a situation or person)
To slap down
To smell a rat
To sniff out
To solve
To sort out (figure out)
To sound the alarm
To sound the charge
To spell out
To squash
To stall
To stand one's ground
To start the ball rolling
To stir (the other person up)
To sum up
To take in (information)
To take stock
To take the wind out of their sails
To take up the challenge
To tap dance (dodge, survive)
To throw down the glove
To throw in the towel
To throw off the covers
To tighten the screws (squeeze)
To tiptoe
To top (other person or previous action)
To trip them up
To undermine
To warn
To weigh up
To whitewash

INDEX

A
accents 29, 30, 31, 57, 61–3, 81
accidents 133–4, 144–5
acrobatics 147, 150
acting 1–2, 24–**35**, 83
 aim of 25–6
 bad 34, 84
 essence of 54
 film 133
 good 34, 52
 Method 31–2
 paragraph 96–7
 styles of 24–5, 32
 vs performing 115
actions **26–7**, 31, 35, 43, 103, 114
 to avoid **42–3**, 77
 colour of **28–9**, 35
 evolve 78–9
 names of 37, 77, 157–8
 objects of 27–8, 31, 35, 39, 43, **55–66**
 playing 34, **36–43**, 53, 57, 83–4, 102
 plotting 74–9
actors 80, 128
 character 109
 personality 109
adjustments 29–30, 31, 35, 43, **55–66**, 103
 minimising 111, 114
 playing 31, 83, 84
 working-in 30, **57–60**
Adler, Stella 31
affectations 31, 58–9
analysis 9, 26, 63, 67–80, 103,
animals and imagery 47, 104, **106**, 114, 142–3, 149, 151, 154
anticipation 83, 84, 89, **94–5**, 119
Armstrong, Louis ix, 128
Armstrong-Jones, Antony 108
art 1, 2, **80**, 100, 112, 125

as if 46–7, 53
audience gravity 118–19, 121–5
audiences 18–19, 20, 22, 25–6, 73, 88–9, 99, **115–27**, 155–6
 bad 126
 dynamics of 80
 film 136–7
 holding 5, 9
 ignoring 141–2
 informing 92–3
 links with 110–11, 144
 as teachers 116
 trial 115
 tricking 95

B
Baitz, Jon Robin 52
Ball, Lucille 122
behaviour 13, **26–31**, 33, 58, 59, 83, 94n, 95, 110
 capsule 143–6
 fake 152
 learning 102
 moments of 116–17
belief 32–33, 45
Benny, Jack 18, 122
Bergman, Ingrid 109
Berkoff, Stephen 56
bigotry 6, 13–14
black humour 8
block 99–100
body 30–1
boredom 5, 23, 44, 81, 88, 89
Boys in the Band, The (Mart Crowley) 1, 138
Brando, Marlon 32, 128, 133–4
Broken Lance, The 103
Brook, Peter 67
Bryant, Michael 67
building a machine 116–17

Burns, George 27–8, 33

C
Caine, Michael 15
caricature **12–14**, 106
cartoons 12, 15, 25
Chaplin, Charles 5, 7, 14, 15, 57, 122, 128
characterisation 100, **102–14**
characters 67, 72–4, 86, 96
 altering 111–12
 emotional journey of 93–4
 personalising 94
 playing 112–13
 spine of 73–4, 93
 stock 108–9
 types of 94
Chekhov, Anton 54, 68
childhood 6–8, 13, 106
 driven humour 7–8, 11–12
children 20, 21, 51, 102, 123, 146
 as actors 58
 see also comedy, the child in
clan, the **10–12**, 13
Clarrie 90–2, 100, 134, 142
classical form 31, 32
Claudius (character, *Hamlet*) 34, 71–2
Claudius (character, *I, Claudius*) 98–9
Claudius the God 98
cliché 61, 108
Clift, Montgomery 89
clubs 44, 88, 90–1
comedy 2, **3–16**, 82, 91
 the child in 6–8

comparison with
    drama 23
  definition of 4
  stand-up 44, 91
  style 14–15
common knowledge
    10–11
common taste 11–12
communication 14, **23**,
    25, 36, 39, 75, 125
concentration **97–8**,
    144, 145, 149,
    152
confusion 5
continuity 130–1
contradiction 15
corners 76, **84–9**, 100,
    101
Costello, Lou 6, 7, 14,
    15
  see also 'Who's On
    First'
Costner, Kevin 102
covers 58–9, 94, 112
Crowley, Mart 1
crying 100
crystallisation 82–84
cues 11, 64, 101, 152
  facial 13, 25
  life- 110, 114
  word 85
culture 1–2, 125–6

D
Dad's Army 109
D'Amato, Gus 36, 43
Danny (character,
    *Sexual Perversity in
    Chicago*) 75–7, 86,
    135
death 8
Deborah (character,
    *Sexual Perversity in
    Chicago*) 75–7, 86,
    135
defence mechanisms
    33, 50, 99
definitions 49
dehumanisation 13
Diary of Anne Frank, The
    47
directors 25, 69, **70–1**,
    72, 79, 115
discipline 30, 32, 36,
    144, 154

discomfort 5–6, 51
disorientation 96
Double Bass 126
double entendres 5
drama 5, 23
  see also timing

E
elegance 32
Eliot, T. S. 139
embarrassment 5, 7
emotional inertia 86–7
emotion memory 49–
    51
emotions 34–5, 49–52,
    98, 148
energy centre 106–8,
    114
Ensemble Theatre 40,
    52
*Epic That Never Was,
    The* (TV
    documentary)
    132
Eponine (character,
    Les Miserables) 69
equilibrium 33–4
Evans, Dame Edith 3,
    83, 88
exaggeration 13, 14
experience 108

F
face pulling 14, 104
faux pas 5
fear 88, 153
feed 9
feelings **15**, 33–4, 42,
    82, 84, 104–5,
    140–1
Fields, W. C. 14
film 24, 25, 49
  and television 115,
    128–37
film stars 32, 102, 109
final thoughts (before
    going on) 152–5
flag, planting a 145
focus 42, 84, 97–8, 132,
    148, 149, 152
follow through 39, 122,
    124
formula 108
Fortinbras (character,
    Hamlet) 72

Fortune and Men's Eyes
    140
Fox (character, *Speed
    the Plow*) 87
Frances (character,
    Travelling North)
    119–23, 135
Frank (character,
    Travelling North)
    119–23, 135
Freddy (character,
    Travelling North)
    120–4
funny acting 14

G
Gallwey, Timothy 65,
    97
Garnett, Alf
    (character) 113
Gertrude (character,
    Hamlet) 32, 46, 93
Ghost, the (character,
    Hamlet) 71, 73–4,
    90, 93
Godfather II, The 110
Gold Rush, The 15
Gordon, Hayes 31, 44,
    78
Gould (character,
    Speed the Plow) 87
Graduate, The 131
graffiti 10
Graves, Robert 98
gravity, centre of 129
guided missiles 38–39,
    43
Gump, Forrest
    (character, *Forrest
    Gump*) 112

H
habit 138, 139
'ham', the 25
Hamlet
  film 68, 72, 90, 93
  play 34, 69, **71–2**, 73,
    93
Hamlet (character) 24,
    32, 46, **71–2**, 73–4,
    90, 93, 140–1
Hanks, Tom 112
Harold (character, *The
    Boys in the Band*) 1,
    138

INDEX

Heathcliff (character, *Wuthering Heights*) 113
Henry IV 145
Hepburn, Katharine 109
hiatus 9, 10, 119
histrionics 32
hitting your mark 133
Hoffman, Dustin 94, 131
holding back 33–5
Hollow Men, The (poem) 139
Hollows, Dr Fred 110
Hollywood 115, 128
homework 81, 125, 131
Homicide 130
homoeostasis 26
Horatio (character, *Hamlet*) 74, 90
Hugo, Victor 69
human nature 11, 80
humiliation 5, 51
humour 7–8, 10–11, 16
Hunchback of Notre Dame, The 113

I

I, Claudius
  film 132
  play 98–99
iambic pentameter 67
identification 80
idiosyncrasies 30, 60, 100, 105, 109
illusion 56–7
imagination 46
imitation 102–5, 114
impersonation 12–14, 106
impersonators 103
imprecision 54
improvisations 40–1, 144
indecision 96
indication 84
inflections 36
inner eye, 106–8
Inner Game, The 65, 97
insight 80
inspiration 80, 108
intellectualisation 51–2
intent 67–8
interaction 80, 116
interactions, real life 80
intimidation 119, 122, 125, 126
intonations 36
Introduction to the Study of Man 1, 26
intuition 80

J

Javert (character, *Les Miserables*) 69
Joey 3, 9, 89
jokes 3, **8–10**, 19–20, 84, 119
  give warning of 122
  in- 11–12
  legitimate stress in 124–5
  risqué 11
  sexually explicit 11
  sharing 123–4
  sick 6
  spelling out 122
Judgement at Nuremberg 103
Juke Box Rhythm 29, 32
just like 47, 49
juxtaposition 15, 19, 91

K

Kaye, Danny 128
Kazan, Elia 133
Keaton, Buster 7, 14, 122
Kramer (character, *Seinfeld*) 83

L

Laertes (character, *Hamlet*) 72, 93
language 14, 90
Last Detail, The 128–9
last note 71–72
last take 134
laughter 2, **3–6**, 10, 116, 118
  killing 123
  pulling back from 121
Laughton, Charles 113, 132
lavatory 6
Le Mesurier, John 109
Les Miserables 69
Lewis, Jerry 3, 14
light bulbs 39, 41, 46
lines 25
  learning 30, 63–4
  speaking 63
Liz (character, *Mother and Son*) 79
loading 46, 96
  up **34–35**, 88, 98, 112, 154–5
location 129–30, 136
logic 8, 80
Lonelyhearts 89
long runs 137, **138–46**
Lowe, Arthur 109

M

Maggie (character, *Mother and Son*) 79
magic **20–1**, 56, 57, 146
Mamet, David 75, 77, 86, 87, 125
mannerisms 30, 31, 35, 57, 105, 109, 110
Marceau, Marcel 25
Marcellus (character, *Hamlet*) 74, 90
Marx, Groucho 6
Marx Brothers 57
Matthau, Walter 128
McKern, Leo 109, 113, 147
memorisation 64, 78
  see also lines, learning
Method approach **31–2**, 39, 58
Midnight Cowboy 94
mimicry 12–14
mimics 30, 103
Misto, John 63, 88
Mitchell, Warren 60, 113
Mitchum, Robert 30, 81, 109
Moment by Moment control 21–2
moments 22, 81–2, 86, 97, 98, 99, 101
  of behaviour 116–17, 143–6
Monroe, Marilyn 128
Montessori, Maria 123
moron, be a 97–8
Mortimer, John 98
Mother and Son 79, 110

motivation 28, 31–2, 35, 39, 43, **44–54**, 149
motivational techniques 44, **45–51**, 53

N
Naked Gun, The 15
naturalism 32
Nicholson, Jack 128–9
Nielsen, Leslie 15
novice actors 58, 142

O
observation 80, 103–4, 114
Olivier, Laurence 25, 68, 72, 90, 91, 93, 113
omission 100
One Man 56
one-person show 47, 56, 63–4, 118, 126–7
On the Waterfront 133
opening night 123, 126
Ophelia (character, *Hamlet*) 34, 72
'other' 6, 13
overview 93–4, 130–1

P
Palace of Dreams 131
pauses 22–3, 88, 118
pay-off 9
perfection 153–4
performances
  colour in 49
  comparing 139–40
  good 55
  preparing 85, 93–4
  style of 31
  texture in 49
performer, becoming a 115
Pericles 57, 91–2
Pericles (character) 91–2
physical
  activities 36
  dexterity 30
  disabilities 14, 103
  errors 5
Picasso 2

Pink Panther, The 15
plant 9, 10
playing
  actions 34, **36–43**, 53, 57, 83–4, 102
  adjustments 31
  colours 29, 83–4, 89
  covers 112
  end results 84, 86, 89
  the form 83, 89, 153
plotting
  actions 74–80
  the journey 93–4
  tips on 77–8
Polonius (character, *Hamlet*) 72
powder keg 10
preparation 97–8, 145–6
Producers, The 15
professionals, observation of 60–1
projection 104–5
pronunciation 11
psychology 25, 31
puns 5, 6, 10, 57

Q
Quasimodo 113
Quinn, Anthony 128
quirks 109, 110

R
realism 25
references **28**, 29, 32, 34, 35, 44, 49–54, 98
rehearsals 80, **81–101**
  film 135–6
rejection 5
repetition 94, 135
reproduction 59, 80
research 60–64
responses 14
Richard III 91
Richards, Michael 83
Richardson, Sir Ralph 46, 71
Richardson, Tony 68, 98
ritual 139–41
Rizzo, Ratso (character, *Midnight Cowboy*) 94
Robert (character, *Mother and Son*) 79, 110

Robertson, Toby 57
Rocco (character, *Sky*) 88
rough, keeping it 95, 100
Rumpole (character, *Rumpole of the Bailey*) 113
Rumpole of the Bailey 109

S
sadism 6
Saint, Eva Marie 133–4
scenes
  core of 135
  natural flow of 134–5
schmaltz 89
scripts 62–4, **67–80**, 89–90
second nights 123
Seinfeld 83
self-consciousness 41–2, 58–9, 147
self-delusion 46
self-honesty 46
Sellers, Peter 14, 15, 83, 132
sense memory 48–9
sequence 130
set-up 9, 19–20
sex 6, 8
Sexual Perversity in Chicago (David Mamet) 75–7
Shakespeare, William 34, 57, 67, 68, 72, 90, 91–3, 125, 140, 145
Shorter, Ken 91
showbusiness 72, 128
simplicity 100, 135
skills 6, 57, 60, 82–3, 138
Sky (John Misto) 63–4, 88, 126–7
social errors 5
sophisticated humour 11
sophistication 11, 21, 22
soul 13–14, 65, 103, 108–9
speeches, long 78, 96
Speed the Plow 87
spine

#INDEX

of characters 72–4, 93
of plays 69–72
scenic 73–4
spontaneity 54, 143–4
Stanislavsky, Konstantin 31
star, being a 126–7
Steady Eddie 14
Stewart, James 109
stimulus 48, 54
Strasberg, Lee 31, 110
stress 124–5
stutterers 105
style 31
  drawing attention to 55–7
Sunshine Boys, The 27
surprise **5**, 54, 84, 117, 122, 123
survival 30
switch 9, 10

T
taboos 6, 8, 11
tags 9, 10, 19–20, 123
Tai Kwan Do 147
Tarzan (character) 128
Tati, Jaques 83
television, film 115, **128–37**
tension **3–4**, 5, 9–10, 11, 12, 47
  breaking the 91–2, 124
Teresa, Mother 110
theatre 23, 32, 56, 57, 128, 129, 131, 137, 143
theatrical conventions 56
Thenardier (character, *Les Miserables*) 69
Third Eye 142–3
thought
  carriers 68
  packages 36–7, 38, 65, 85
  sequences 64, 78, 86, 131
Three Hotels (Jon Robin Baitz) 52, 144
Three Stooges, The 57
timing 16, **17–23**, 45, 86, 98, 113
  and audiences 116
  in drama 8–9, 23
  essence of 18
  in film and television 115
  fundamental ingredient of 5
  good 125
  inner and outer 17
  instinctive 85
  over- and under- 19–20
  see also jokes
toilet 8
Tracy, Spencer 103, 109, 110
tragedy 91
transactional analysis 31
transcendental meditation 147
Travelling North 119, 129, 147
Tree of Man, The 66
tricks 108–9
truth 15–16, 59, 80, 90–2, 124, 137, 155–6
type, playing against 109–10
type casting 30

U
uncertainty 118

usury 45–6, 47, 53

V
Valjean, Jean (character, *Les Miserables*) 69
verbal errors 5
voice 30–1
vowel sounds 62, 103, 105

W
walk 103, 106–8
  pregnant 108
warming up 31, 145–6, **147–56**
Warner, David 98–9
watching 2, 42, 51
wedges 88, 95–6, 100
Weissmuller, Johnny 128
West, Mae 14, 122
White, Matt 44, 47
White, Patrick 66
'Who's On First?' (sketch, Abbott and Costello) 7n
Wilder, Gene 15
Wild One, The 32
Williamson, David 119, 122
will vs skill 36
Without a Clue 15
words 36, 62–6, **67–8**
Wuthering Heights 113

Y
Yes, Minister 11–12
Young, Dr J. Z. 1, 26, 125

Z
Zeffirelli, Franco 68